*PÁLL BALDVIN
BALDVINSSON*

ICELAND
INVADED

THE ALLIED OCCUPATION
IN WORLD WAR II

JPV ÚTGÁFA

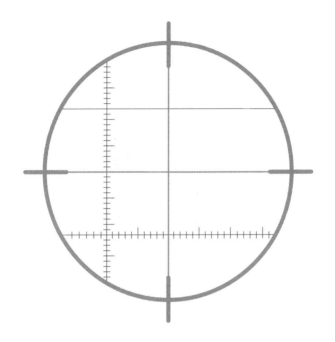

ICELAND INVADED
The Allied Occupation in World War II

© Páll Baldvin Baldvinsson 2019
English translation © Lorenza Garcia 2019

JPV útgáfa • Reykjavík • 2019

Layout and cover design: Halla Sigga / Forlagið
Main font: Garamond BE 9.7/14 pt
Cover Photo: NARA 80-G-24831
Printing: Prentmiðlun / Latvia

Published in Reykjavík, a UNESCO City of Literature

ISBN 978-9935-11-882-0

JPV útgáfa is an imprint of ⟨⟩ Forlagið ehf.
www.forlagid.is

On the eve of May 10 1940, four darkened battleships steamed north towards the white isle: the destroyers HMS Fearless and HMS Fortune occupied the flank positions, and between them two cruisers from His Majesty's Naval Service, HMS Glasgow and HMS Berwick. The ships had put out to sea in the early hours of May 8. On board were approximately 800 men, among them privates, officers, members of the British intelligence and diplomatic services. Two days earlier, Winston Churchill had decided on behalf of the British Government that the occupation of Iceland must take place without delay.

Conditions on board were wretched. The troops were unaccustomed to travelling by sea, and many suffered terrible seasickness. Shortly before reaching Reykjavík harbour, they were given a meal of sausages and hot chocolate. The skies were overcast, it was cold, and there was patchy rain. A young recruit called John Shelley disappeared beneath a tarpaulin and fired the first shot (and his last) of the occupying forces. A farewell letter to his mother was found in his pocket.

The leaders of the invasion were ill-prepared: the son of a Newcastle merchant, who knew his way around Reykjavík, drew a map of the city; a Classics master at Eton College, who came frequently to Iceland for the salmon fishing, struggled to compose a speech addressed to the Icelandic people in their native tongue. The occupying force's military equipment dated from the Great War. That night the war took on a new appearance. The Germans launched surprise attacks on Belgium, Holland and Luxembourg. The Allies were fighting German invasion forces in Norway. Ships carrying Norwegian refugees landed in east Iceland. Iceland's repeatedly declared neutrality was hanging by a thread. The British Army would soon be in the streets of Reykjavík.

The war in Europe, which began with Germany's invasion of Poland in the early hours of September 1 1939, spread to Scandinavia in the spring, when, on April 9 1940, the German army invaded Denmark and Norway. The invasion came as no surprise: the Icelandic delegation in Copenhagen were convinced it was only a matter of time, and six days earlier, on April 3, the Standing Committee on Foreign Affairs had discussed the risk of war in the Icelandic parliament. On April 5, Reykjavík newspapers reported the amassing of German troops.

People in Akureyri, in the north of Iceland, are reading the morning newspapers from Reykjavík on the of August 30 1939.

King Christian X, the last in a long line of monarchs to reign over Iceland. His brother, Haakon, was the king of Norway.

British and German radio stations were quick to broadcast news of the invasion. The Reykjavík newspapers published a bulletin the following morning, and updated their news reports, as events unfolded. Radio in Iceland had limited reach.

Early on April 9, the Icelandic government called meetings with the Standing Committee on Foreign Affairs and the political parties in parliament. According to Iceland's constitution, the Danish king was the highest authority in the land. For the past eight hundred years, Iceland had been jointly under the rule of the Danish and Norwegian crowns. The Danish king currently presided over an occupied country, and his powers were limited; all communications with Denmark had been cut off.

Kallio, the Finnish prime minister, King Haakon V of Norway, King Gustaf V of Sweden and King Christian X of Iceland and Denmark attended a historic meeting in Stockholm of the Nordic heads of state in October 1939, in which they affirmed their countries' neutrality.

That same morning, the British government decided to make a formal request to the Icelandic government to provide facilities for its army and navy. The petition arrived in the late afternoon, while parliament was debating the question of the Danish king's authority, and whether or not Iceland should seize control of its own foreign affairs. Britain's desire for a military base on Icelandic soil was now an open secret. The meeting ended at three o'clock in the morning, with a unanimous cross-party decision to end 800 years of European dynastic rule in Iceland.

The following day, the British request was politely refused: Iceland was a neutral country.

The years leading up to the war had tested this neutrality. Whoever ruled Iceland was in control of the North Atlantic Ocean. Successive Icelandic governments had adhered to the neutrality of the Nordic nations, which had enabled them during WWI to sell food and raw materials to the opposing powers.

The Great Depression arrived late in Iceland, although the years after 1930 saw a slump in the price of fish. The Spanish Civil War brought far greater losses, as exports of salt fish to Spain ceased entirely. Germany and Great Britain were both important markets for Icelandic trade. During WWI, the British created a blockade around Iceland and applied economic sanctions to the country. Over the centuries, Germany and Iceland had enjoyed good relations, both commercially and culturally, and both Great Britain and Germany had their supporters in Iceland. In the years leading up to the war, Iceland, whose economy was stagnating, had made unsuccessful attempts to persuade the British and the Germans to sign trade agreements, and to extend further credit to the country.

Still photograph of Eva Braun taken during her trip to Iceland in 1938.

The German nation was greatly interested in Iceland: German cruise boats would often visit the island, and the two countries frequently competed in sporting events. German pilots, many

German U-boats at Reykjavík harbour, U-26 and U-27, under the command of Admiral Hans-Georg von Friedeburg, he would be remembered in history for signing the surrender of the Germany forces in Northern Germany, Holland and Denmark to the 21st Army Group led by Field Marshal Montgomery on May 4 1945.

directly linked to the Luftwaffe and the SS, offered gliding lessons to Icelandic enthusiasts. Several scientists from the Ahnenerbe, the SS research group, made expeditions to Iceland to conduct research in various fields. Welcoming parties would greet German training ships and U-boats arriving in Reykjavík harbour. German men, many of whom were self-professed Nazis, lived and worked all over Iceland. During the same period, number of German refugees sought asylum in Iceland. Some had been exiled because of their political views, others because of their ethnic background. The Icelandic authorities followed the policy of the other Nordic countries, and as a result dozens of refugees were turned away from Iceland's shores and hundreds were refused asylum. Documents show that many of them would later become victims of the Holocaust.

*The Rosenthals – a family from Berlin settled in Reykjavík and
Akureyri in the prewar years. Part of the family stayed on and perished in Auschwitz and Natzweiler Struthof in 1943. The photo
is taken on the first documented Yom Kippur in Iceland in september 1940. Attending are British soldiers and members of
the Rosenthals and the Zeizel-family that fled from Vienna.*

LUFTHANSA REQUESTS
LANDING RIGHTS

In the nineteen twenties, foreign commercial airlines expressed
an interest in scheduling flights to Iceland. From the early thirties
up until April 1 1940, the German state airline Lufthansa enjoyed
the most favourable landing rights for scheduled flights to Iceland.

Flying was the future solution for a country with no road network, where the few vehicles in existence were confined to urban
areas. In 1938, the first airline to run scheduled flights in a float-
plane had been founded; the airfields in Iceland were rudimen-
tary. Plans were made to drain swampland and build an airfield
– where the current airport is situated in the centre of Reykjavík.

In March 1939, representatives of Lufthansa arrived in Reykjavík to discuss the airline's landing rights. News of this was published in a Danish newspaper, and the story broke the same day in Reykjavík. In the US media, there were reports of plans to build a German submarine base in Iceland. The German training ship, SMS Emden, was expected to arrive in Reykjavík at any moment. Czechoslovakia had recently fallen into Nazi hands. Hitler was in Vienna. Would Iceland be next?

When a member of the Icelandic parliament, and editor of a socialist newspaper, asked the prime minister whether SMS Emden's arrival was connected to Lufthansa's request, he didn't receive a clear answer. He promptly sent a telegram to a communist newspaper in Copenhagen, informing them that the German authorities were using the arrival of SMS Emden to put pressure on Iceland with regard to landing rights – the news spread to the other western nations, and was seen as proof of the Third Reich's encroachment on Europe.

Hermann Jónasson's government cleverly managed to get themselves out of this bind by making Lufthansa's landing rights contingent on the scheduled flights of other airlines to Iceland, and so the German request died a natural death: "... the increasing uncertainty and agitation in world affairs ... is the motive for the government's position". The rebuff was duly noted by the rest of the world.

In May 1939 a new German Consul was appointed to Iceland: Dr Werner Gerlach. He was a close associate of Himmler and Göring, and a member of the Nazi party. The Nordic descendants of the Vikings were a disappointment to him, and everywhere he could detect the influence of Jews on the nation's culture. He wished to house the consulate in a building worthy of the Third Reich, and, with Himmler's help, received funds from the SS to purchase a villa in Túngata.

Not long afterwards, a British training ship sailed into Reykjavík harbour. On board was an envoy of the British government, Berkeley Gage. He had been sent there to find out what the Icelandic authorities thought about the increasing activity of the Third Reich. His report was filed to the Foreign Office.

Lionel Fortescue, a British patriot and Classics master at Eton College, spent that summer in Iceland. He travelled to the country every year for the salmon fishing, and had a smattering of Icelandic. The previous spring, he had met with British Naval Intelligence, and offered to travel to Iceland to set up a spy network that would monitor the movements of German ships and U-boats to and from the island. At the end of the summer, he had a meeting with the chairman of the Standing Committee on Foreign Affairs in the Icelandic parliament, and together they established a network of forty Icelanders spying for the British in different locations around the island.

The German Vice Consul's emblem.

Dr Werner Gerlach at his bureau in Reykjavík. For the purposes of the photograph, a portrait of Hitler was removed, along with other signs of Gerlach's regard for the Nazi leadership and its ideology.

When war broke out, Fortescue became stranded in Iceland and didn't get home until November, when he filed his report on the spy ring to the British authorities.

In August 1939, a German trawler arrived in Iceland. Two young Germans disembarked, one a meteorologist, the other a radio operator. They both worked for the Consul Gerlach. They moved into the new consulate, where they set up a radio transmitter that sent encrypted messages to Germany. These included weather reports and information on the movements of British vessels, the first of which was a destroyer sailing off the coast of Vestmannaeyjar at the end of September 1939. By then, rumours of a clandestine German radio transmitter were already circulating in Reykjavík.

The German ship SS Arucas (3,359 grt) was intercepted by HMS York 50 miles off the southeast of Iceland. The crew scuttled the ship in a gale force 9. Three drowned but 39 of the crew were saved by HMS York.

Gerlach breathed new life into the social life of Germans residing in Reykjavík, and of Icelandic Germanophiles. During that period, all things German were associated with the Nazi regime. Icelanders were aware of this from reading the British and Scandinavian press. The photograph was taken at Hótel Borg in Reykjavík in January 1940, and shows preparations for a party organised by Germania, a society for the promotion of friendship between Iceland and Germany.

THE WEATHER REPORTS

Since Iceland became connected to mainland Europe and America by cable and pylon at the beginning of the century, Icelandic weather reports had become indispensable to weather forecasting in the Atlantic Ocean. Ten weather reports were broadcast daily from Iceland, and these were picked up by merchant ships and fishing vessels from various different countries navigating the North Atlantic. Meteorologists all over Europe used the information contained in these reports for their forecasting. During WWI, the British used their influence to ensure that Icelandic weather reports were sent by cable, to hinder the enemy's ability to undertake sea voyages. During WWII, six of the ten daily weather reports were transmitted by radiogram, and four weather reports were broadcast over the radio in Icelandic, English, and German. Once again, the British requested that weather reports be sent by cable to prevent interception by the Germans. The Icelandic prime minister announced that radio broadcasts of weather reports in English and German were to be discontinued, and would instead be sent by mail to the British and German consuls.

Amateur radio operators in Reykjavík started picking up strange messages. This came to the attention of the French consul, who informed the British Consul. The British Consul then requested a search be carried out to locate the secret transmitter.

Up until late December 1939, two men were employed in shifts to send encrypted weather reports to the Germany Navy from the attic of the German consulate. By then, the Icelandic authorities had zeroed in on the transmitter, and were able to verify its location by cutting off the electricity supply to the consul's house while a message was being sent, thus interrupting the transmission in mid-stream.

With the outbreak of war, the government imposed rationing in Iceland. The shortages during the Great War were fresh in people's memory. The supplies of hops and wholesalers were inventoried, and freight charges were raised on October 1 1939. A week later, sailors negotiated a risk premium, referred to as "scare money". The British ordered that all vessels sailing to the British Isles dock at Kirkwall in the Orkneys to have their cargo inspected.

Already in September, numerous German, Norwegian, Danish and Swedish vessels had requested permission to dock in Reykjavík harbour. British warships were navigating the Icelandic fishing banks in search of German merchant vessels. On September 24, the SS Minden (a 431 grt German cargo vessel) was scuppered by her crew when the British cruiser HMS Calypso intercepted her off the southeast coast of Iceland. Then the British captured the 13,615 grt German Liner SS Cap Norte off the west coast of Iceland. During that first autumn of the war, the Royal Navy hunted down German ships off the Icelandic coast. Some escaped, others were scuppered by their crew, and still others were captured or sunk by the British. The last German vessel to leave Reykjavík harbour on October 18 1939 was captured two days later by the British.

The Icelandic authorities began to appreciate the ruthlessness of the belligerent parties: the Soviet attack on Finland in November 1939 was strongly condemned in Iceland, and the socialist group was isolated in parliament, leading to a split in their party. Icelandic diplomats were alarmed; the Icelandic consul in New York urged Prime Minister Hermann Jónasson to request military protection from the United States, which had declared its neutrality. This could not be seen to constitute a threat to the balance of power in the western Atlantic. The consul was charged with finding out how the US authorities felt about protecting Iceland militarily.

An Icelandic delegation to London stayed for eight weeks in December 1939. The price of fish was rising steeply, British trawlers had been seconded to the navy, and by the end of 1939 the British fishing fleet had lost 122 of its vessels. Britain realised the importance of protecting shipments of fish, herring, fish liver oil and fishmeal from Iceland, which the Ministry of Agriculture, Fisheries and Food considered an essential part of the nation's food supplies.

The chairman of the delegation, Ambassador Sveinn Björnsson, was summoned to a private meeting at the Foreign Office on

December 11. The Head of the Northern Section, Laurence Collier, asked him a direct question: would Iceland provide facilities for the Royal Navy and Air Force in the event of a German attack on Denmark? Sveinn responded by asking whether the British would occupy Iceland by force if they refused. How did Collier think the Americans would respond if Iceland were to be invaded by either the British or the Germans?

Following this meeting, Sveinn sent a memorandum to the Icelandic government.

VISITS FROM U-BOATS AND SEAPLANES

When hostilities broke out, the neutral Nordic countries established rules governing the landing of warships and aircraft on their shores. The Soviet Union flouted Finnish neutrality, and that of Iceland was put to the test a few weeks into the war.

On the eve of September 4 1939, a German U-boat, U-30, torpedoed and sank the British transatlantic liner, SS Athenia. The Germans denied responsibility for the attack, which caused a stir internationally.

When the same U-boat attacked the British cargo steamship, SS Fanad Head, the crew radioed for assistance. The Fanad Head was captured, and the crew placed in lifeboats. A German crew was sent aboard to sink her. The distress call had been intercepted by the British aircraft carrier, HMS Ark Royal, which sent three Skua aircraft to the scene. Three destroyers were also detached to assist SS Fanad Head. Two of the Skuas bombed the U-boat, which lay alongside the Fanad Head, but were hit by shrapnel from their own bombs and crashed into the sea. Two airmen managed to swim to the SS Fanad Head, where three members of the German crew had been wounded. The British airmen were captured, and all five men were taken aboard the U-boat, which was now under attack by a Swordfish bi-plane sent from HMS Ark Royal. One of the Germans, Adolf Schmidt, had a ruptured artery, and was taken to the nearest safe harbour, in Reykjavík. The U-boat arrived on September 19 carrying the two British prisoners hidden on board and the wounded German crew members.

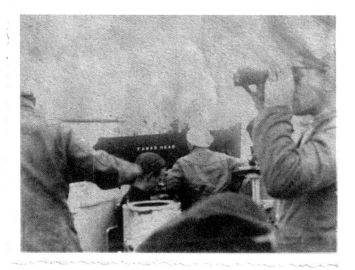

The capture of Fanad Head from the deck of U-30.

Gerlach requested permission from the port authorities for Schmidt to be taken onto land, and he treated the two other wounded men himself. The authorities threatened to commandeer the U-30. Schmidt was taken onto land, where he would remain in custody for the duration of the war. The first mate on a German merchant vessel moored in Reykjavík harbour managed to get on board the U-boat, and smuggled some maps Gerlach had passed to him. Before they allowed Schmidt onto land, he was sworn to secrecy over the U-30's attack on the SS Athenia two weeks earlier. He kept quiet until the end of the war, after which he disclosed details of the attack. His witness statement was presented at the Nuremberg Trials. The two British airmen spent the remainder of the war in a German prison camp.

In the week following the visit by the U-30, the first warplane touched down in Iceland. It was a Catalina seaplane – one of the first aircraft supplied to the RAF by the United States. The aircraft was on a reconnaissance and test flight when bad weather forced it to land at Raufarhöfn, in the northeasternmost corner of Iceland. The nine crewmembers decided to wait until the weather improved. The authorities grounded the plane, and a police officer was hurriedly flown up from Reykjavík, carrying a submachine gun in his luggage. He was set down in the nearest village, and rode on horseback overnight to Raufarhöfn. Later the next day, he met with the captain of the Catalina. Captain Barnes gave his word of honour to respect the grounding of the aircraft, and was permitted to call the British consul. The consul had already spoken to London, who saw only two ways out: the crew could either respect the grounding order, or attempt to get away.

Barnes returned to the plane, ordered the propellers to be started, and took off. The aircraft made one more landing near Vatnsnes in the north before heading to the British Isles.

The seaplane incident attracted international criticism. The Danish authorities protested, and Berlin and Moscow radio stations announced that the British disrespected the neutrality of small nations. The Icelandic authorities demanded that Captain Barnes take responsibility for his actions. Finally, he was sent back Iceland and put under house arrest at Bessastaðir. He was recently married, and his wife was permitted to follow him. They were supposed to share the accommodation with Adolf Schmidt, but the German objected, and was subsequently moved to Reykjavík.

Dr. Gerlach and Adolf Schmidt in Reykjavík harbour.

On January 3 1940, the British government sent a message to Iceland, which was forwarded to the Danish authorities on January 18. In it, the British made a secret offer of military protection to Iceland. The Icelandic ambassador discussed the matter with King Christian X in the presence of the Danish prime minister, and the message was then encrypted and sent back to Reykjavík. In early February, Iceland refused the British offer of military protection.

The Icelandic consul in New York was still working towards requesting United States military protection for Iceland. Around the same time, a memo sent by the explorer Vilhjálmur Stefánsson, who was of Icelandic descent, to Secretary of State Cordell Hull appeared in the American press. Stefánsson affirmed that if Iceland fell into enemy hands, it would be used as a springboard for an attack on the States.

Captain Barnes plane in Raufarhöfn.

During that time, German warships were being captured in large numbers off the coast of Iceland. Crews were under orders to scupper their vessels rather than leave them in the hands of the British. The Germans sank three Nordic ships at the end of January 1940. The big battle cruisers HMS Scharnhorst, and HMS Gneisenau patrolled the Denmark Strait, which was the route taken by German merchant vessels heading for German ports. One of those vessels, the cargo ship SS Bahia Blanca, hit an ice floe, and started taking on water. The sixty-two-man crew bailed out into rough seas, and were rescued by an Icelandic trawler, which brought them to land. Rumours spread that they were undercover agents, sent to prepare the way for a German invasion of Iceland.

On April 3 1940, The Royal Navy produced a report about Iceland's strategic importance as a naval base. The report was sent to Winston Churchill and Admiral of the Fleet Sir Dudley Pound, who both initialled it.

On the previous day, Hitler had instructed his army to invade Denmark and Norway on the morning of April 9.

With the invasion of Denmark, all telephone contact between Copenhagen and Iceland ceased. Almost immediately, employees at the Icelandic national telephone exchange reported that the transmitter in the German consulate had resumed its activities after a four-month silence. Two German men were responsible for those transmissions. One was in a relationship with the daughter of a hotel owner in Reykjavík, and the other was a drinking companion of the British Vice-Consul Hoblyn, a Germanophile, whose previous posting was Hamburg. This friendship had been struck up at the instigation of Gerlach.

During the days that followed, the transmissions increased, and on April 14, the British demanded that action be taken. A search of the consul's residence would have been a bold step, as the building was legally on German soil. A Social Democrat minister objected to the plan, and the chief of police was ordered to call off the search. The following day, April 20, was Hitler's birthday. The chief of police paid Gerlach a visit, informed him that the Icelandic authorities were aware of the radio transmitter's existence, and ordered him to cease all transmissions. Gerlach was offended, insisting there was no such transmitter on the premises.

The chief of police had been invited to Germany by Himmler in the summer of 1939 to learn about German policing practices, and he spoke German. He would later end up on a British register of Germany's friends in Iceland. He told Gerlach in no uncertain terms that the radio signal had been repeatedly picked up, and reiterated that all transmissions of encrypted messages to Germany must cease.

The young and newly appointed chief of police in Reykjavík, Agnar Kofoed-Hansen, on a shooting range with officers from KRIPO in the summer of 1939 on invitation from Himmler.

The following day, the British Foreign Office suggested to the Icelandic government that they deport all German nationals. Several days later, the British government invited Iceland to appoint representatives to London, and informed them that a British ambassador would soon be appointed to Iceland. This amounted to a British recognition of Iceland as an independent state.

On the morning of May 9 1940, the British consul in Reykjavík was informed that at 17h00 a coded dispatch would arrive from the British government. Vice-Consul Hoblyn passed this information to his German drinking companion. When the dispatch arrived, the British consul left his residence and deciphered the message: the following morning, His Majesty's Royal Marines would invade Iceland. The invasion was planned for 5h00; an advance guard would go directly to the German consul's residence, and others would take over the post office and the telephone exchange, and block all roads in and out of Reykjavík.

A few days earlier, a son had been born to Vice-Consul Hoblyn. Under the guise of celebrating the birth of the child, invitations to a cocktail party at the consul's residence in Höfða were sent out, in preparation for the arrival of the invasion forces. Eight people were present, amongst them Captain Barnes and his wife. After holding a toast, the consul informed the company that Iceland would be invaded by morning. The men then drew up plans for the arrest of German nationals, and the seizure of houses and land for officers and men. The party continued into the night, while they awaited the arrival of the British fleet.

It is two o'clock in the morning, and four battleships are sailing across Faxaflói towards Reykjavík. From one of them, a Walrus biplane takes off to patrol the city. The inhabitants are sound asleep, but the plane flies low, and people all over the city are woken by the noise. A German musician on his way home from work calls the German consul. Gerlach is already up, having driven down to the harbour that night to scour the horizon for ships. Ministers are roused, and everywhere people are getting up from their beds. At 3h40 the ships are sighted, and the Wal-

Troops leave HMS Berwick for HMS Fearless.

rus biplane continues to circle above the city. A night watchman informs the police, and a crowd of people gathers at the harbour. Troops are moved between ships, and HMS Fearless sails full speed into the harbour, where she moors, and a stream of troops disembarks. Consul General Shepherd welcomes Major Quill, who heads the intelligence team. Escorted by thirty troops, the two men set off for the German consul's residence. Gerlach has been busy making calls all over town to alert his fellow Germans. He, his wife and their maid are busy carrying documents up to the first floor bathroom to burn them. Then comes a knock at the door: *Nicht aufmachen*, he commands. A voice orders him to open the door. Gerlach goes down, and asks Shepherd what he wants. The consul wishes to enter. We are on neutral territory here, Gerlach protests. Denmark was also neutral, retorts Shepherd, and the house is taken by force.

Dr Gerlach with his walking stick is escorted to a car. Behind him is his daughter. Following is her mother and a maid of the house.

Dr. Gerlach was the last to sit in the car, with his wife's fur coat on his arm. He tried to hide a pistol from his captors.

During the rest of that day, supplies and equipment were unloaded. German citizens were detained in guesthouses, as well as in their homes, dragged from the arms of spouses and children, some never to return. In the late afternoon, they were herded together on the quayside and taken by boat to Berwick. None of those detained put up any resistance to the soldiers, or were found to be carrying weapons, except for Gerlach, who tried to smuggle a pistol on board when he and his wife and daughters were taken to the ship. His younger daughter was upset, because she supposed to have a birthday party later that day.

The Icelandic government held a meeting at 10h00. The British commanders were getting themselves ready at the city's finest hotel. Dressed in suits, they were driven by car the short distance to the ministry offices, where they stepped out and donned their top hats. Heading the group was the newly appointed ambassador, Howard Smith. Scarcely a month earlier, the Germans had detained Smith in Copenhagen, and he and his staff were taken by truck to an awaiting ship. Now he was in Iceland, accompanied by the head of the trade commission C. R. S. Harris, General Consul Shepherd, and Lionel Fortescue, the Classics master at Eton College. All over Reykjavík, people were laughing at the wording of Fortescue's letter, which he had drafted on the journey north, and which had been circulated to the population.

The Government waited. Prime Minister Hermann Jónasson embraced Fortescue as he would an old friend, but otherwise his manner was brusque. Ambassador Smith presented the prime minister with his credentials in the form of a letter from King George VI addressed to King Christian X of Denmark, reading "My dear friend and cousin". Hermann Jónasson accepted the letter. Smith then informed him that, notwithstanding Iceland's neutrality, British troops were occupying the island to secure a base for their naval and air patrols. He referred to the longstanding friendship between their two countries, and assured him that the British had no intention of meddling in Iceland's internal affairs. They simply wished to support the Icelandic economy, and to promote trade between the two countries. Hermann Jónasson considered the army's presence unnecessary, and made clear his opposition. In the report he sent to London later that day, Ambassador Smith described the meeting as brief but cordial. Iceland issued a formal protest by telephone that evening at 18h00. At the time, the Government was attending an informal meeting over a glass of whisky with Ambassador Smith at Hótel Borg. That evening, the Icelandic prime minister addressed the Icelandic population over the radio. He referred to the British Army as guests, and asked that they be treated with the utmost courtesy.

The expedition to Iceland had been arranged in a hurry, and approximately 300 tons of provisions and equipment had been left behind. The 2nd Division of Marines took Reykjavík, and on May 13 further reinforcements were due to set sail, with replacement troops arriving on May 27. The British paid hired lorries, buses and taxis to transport soldiers around the city, and trucks of varying sizes to carry equipment to the camps. The first barracks were installed on a large open space to the south of the city, where

The occupying force with admirers the first morning.

A Lewis set up at 7h50 for opposition by the Salvation Army headquarters. On the left a lady can not hide her disdain.

Raising the tents the first evening. Groups of children followed the preparations.

the national library and museum are currently situated. Official buildings were requisitioned by the army: schools, gymnasiums, and halls of residence at the university were turned into hospitals, Hótel Borg was reserved for the top brass, and the national theatre, which was still under construction, was used to store provisions.

The occupation commenced on the Friday before Whitsun: the fishing season had just ended, and the schools holidays were about to begin. Inquisitive residents surrounded the soldiers, and when evening came, young people, especially girls, emerged in droves.

Soldiers were taken by coach to Selfoss in the east, and from there down to Kaldaðarnes, on the banks of the Ölfus River. Captain Barnes considered the firm riverbank a good location for an airfield. They arrived to find a crowd gathered. At first, the soldiers were confused, but a local farmer – the only person there who spoke some English, was able to enlighten them: he owned the surrounding land, but had recently retired, and was auctioning off his livestock.

A station for glider pilots at Sandskeiði on May 11. Two years earlier teachers from the Luftwaffe were stationed there to train young Icelandic enthusiasts in glide flying.

The day after, on Saturday morning, Ambassador Smith and Consul Shepherd knocked on the door of the ministry offices. The concierge informed them that it was a national holiday and the building was empty. That day, a meeting of the British and Icelandic trade commissions was held, and an air defence force was set up. Soldiers transported anti-aircraft guns from the harbour and located them in strategic positions around the city; no matter how antiquated their weaponry, Sturges wanted the army's defences up and running.

The people of Reykjavík hurry as the reinforcements arrive. A Sunderland flies over the city.

Reinforcements arrived on May 17. Instead of the expected 147 brigades comprised of 2,500 troops under the command of General George Lammie, 3,728 men and women arrived, including engineers, artisans and nursing staff. The soldiers were now dispersed to Hafnarfjörður, Akureyri and Seyðisfjörður. Lammie soon realised that his troops alone could not defend Iceland's rugged, sparsely populated coastline. Smith's request for more men was denied, and the British military authorities even considered calling men back from Iceland to bolster Britain's own defences. A request for reinforcements was made to the Canadian government. Rumoured sightings of German ships in the sea between Norway and Iceland caused widespread alarm. The Allies' retreat from Norway was at its peak, and German warships were on the hunt for fleeing vessels: on June 8 the Germans sank three troop carriers with a loss of 1,515 men. Eight days later RMS Andania was sunk off the Icelandic coast, and an Icelandic trawler saved the lives of 350 men from the steamship. That same day, Canadian reinforcements arrived in Reykjavík. The allied troops at Dunkirk had escaped, and France had fallen into Germany's hands.

*The Bathhouse mid-town Reykjavík was popular
from the first week of the occupation, but the soldiers
had to leave their weapons outside while they showered.*

Iceland's ambassador to Denmark, Sveinn Björnsson, was recalled after the Germans invaded Denmark. He obtained permission from Berlin to return home, and set sail from Genoa. Danish engineers had been commissioned to design the heating system under preparation in Reykjavík, and their technical drawings were delivered to the ambassador just before his departure. He arrived in New York on May 9, and awoke the following day to the news that Iceland had been occupied. Sveinn had brought with him a secret message from the physicist Niels Bohr, and on day one of his two-day stopover in the city, he met with the Danish ambassador, Henrik Kaufmann. Kaufmann was the only Danish diplomat who openly opposed Germany's occupation of Denmark on April 9. He presented Sveinn Björnsson with all the files from the Danish embassy's Department of Icelandic Affairs. Kaufmann then began immediate negotiations with the US Government regarding the defence of Greenland and access to its cryolite mines – cryolite being a mineral that was vital to the production of aluminium used in aircraft construction. Sveinn Björnsson returned to Reykjavík on May 22, and took up a post as a government advisor. With him arrived Bertil Eric Kuniholm, the new US consul.

Further reinforcements arrived on June 26: 2,800 troops under the command of Major-General H.O. Curtis. The men had recently been evacuated from Dunkirk, and their morale was low. They were deployed to small towns and villages around the country. The British troops were made up of recruits, while the Canadians were volunteers, of all types, including a few bad apples. All of them were old enough to have seen the effects of the Great War on the minds and bodies of their fathers, cousins, and neighbours; they realised that this sojourn in Iceland was a moment of relative peace.

A Canadian post at Kambabrún near Hveragerði.

The British troops were generally well liked. It was common for women to do their laundry for them, as well as deliveries that had to be made on time, and friendships were often formed between the troops and local families. The soldiers' diet was monotonous, and they would often barter with the local population – cigarettes or money in exchange for eggs and milk. The daily wage of a private was two-shillings and ninepence, while that of a colonel was two pounds and nine shillings. The class difference between a private and a commanding officer was conspicuous.

On July 3, reports came through of a German U-boat sinking a large passenger ship – the SS Arandora Star, which had once brought summer guests to Iceland and had been requisitioned at the beginning of the war. At the time of the attack, she was transporting 1,500 prisoners of war from Great Britain to Canada. On the ship were some of the Germans who had originally been deported from Iceland, two of whom lost their lives. On board another prisoner ship bound for Australia, HMT Dunera,

A lady doing the washing for soldiers at Borgarnes.

Soldiers fooling around with children.

was a German soap manufacturer from Akureyri. The majority of Germans detained by the British in Iceland were sent to a prison camp on the Isle of Man in the autumn of 1940, where they remained for several years.

Every week, Icelandic trawlers would set sail for the British Isles with shipments of fish, and weekly convoys carrying supplies and troops sailed between the two countries. The German U-boat fleet was making forays into the northernmost corner of the Atlantic. In the summer, a British ship laid a row of mines from the east coast of Iceland to the Faroe Islands, and onwards to the Orkneys. This was aimed at preventing the German fleet from gaining easy access to the area of ocean off Iceland's south coast. Mines were also laid from the north west coast of Iceland to Greenland. Reports of minelaying appeared in the Reykjavík newspapers. In the summer of 1940 a German aircraft sank a British trawler off the East Fjords.

Promophoto from the British.

At the time, Germany was considering plans to invade Great Britain and Iceland. However, Hitler was advised that transporting troops and supplies to Iceland would be complicated. The planned attacks were abandoned, and Hitler's attentions turned to his campaign in the east.

In Iceland, British commanders anticipated the worst, and had made preparations to declare martial law. They informed the Icelandic authorities, who agreed these should be implemented in the event of an attack.

In August, blackouts were ordered in urban areas, and social gatherings were prohibited. Underage girls, known by the Reykjavík police to be involved with soldiers, were increasingly put under surveillance. Prostitution did occur, and young girls would sometimes exchange affections for gifts or money.

In the autumn, lighthouses were switched off along the coast, much to the frustration of sailors, and the army built lookout posts in various locations to follow shipping and U-boat activity. Trawlers sailing to the British Isles with cargoes of fish would often pick up people cast adrift in lifeboats or from sinking ships. The most spectacular exploit involved the crew of two trawlers, who rescued 620 men from a burning troop carrier in the Irish Sea.

The occupation was beginning to have an effect on the local economy: there were water shortages in Reykjavík, the autumn potato harvest was being stockpiled by individuals, and as housing was in short supply, the authorities passed laws capping rents. There was an increase in the circulation of money, as well as frequent price increases for goods and services.

The British constructed an airfield on the Kaldaðarnes plain, where the 18 Fairey Battle aircraft that had arrived in August were kept. This was the first formation to fly across the ocean from the British Isles. However, the aircraft didn't perform well, and was phased out. In early October, the first German reconnaissance flight over Iceland took place when a German Heinkel aircraft flew over Reykjavík and Kaldaðarnes.

British cargo transports travelling from the east coast of the United States and from Canada in large convoys increasingly came under attack by German U-boats. The shipping route lay just off the south coast of Iceland. Every week, dozens of merchant seamen were lost.

The expanding labour market led to a general strike at the beginning of 1941. Two British soldiers, who were communist sympathisers, composed a speech in English urging their fellow soldiers to disobey orders. The strikers circulated the pamphlet among the barracks. The perpetrators were found and arrested by the military police. They received a prison sentence, but the identity of the authors of the leaflet was never discovered. This affair led to the laws on treason and the sabotage of army property being tightened. The military intelligence services kept a file on Icelandic sailors, and workers who held radical views were blacklisted.

BREAKING AWAY

At the beginning of the New Year 1941, the British government raised the matter of Iceland dissolving the 1918 Danish-Icelandic Act of Union. However, it was feared that by unilaterally abandoning the agreement they would give grist to the German propaganda mill. The voices of those who believed that the war justified postponing the decision were still relatively silent. Sveinn Björnsson led talks with the British ambassador, Howard Smith. He informed Smith of his government's attempts to persuade the Americans to take over the military defence of the country. US Ambassador Kuniholm met twice with the Icelandic foreign minister, and passed on a message from Roosevelt's Secretary of State, Cordell Hull: if the situation arose, the US must be given a free hand in Iceland.

Another meeting took place between Sveinn Björnsson and Ambassador Smith, after which Sveinn Björnsson concluded that the British and Americans were undoubtedly elaborating their own plans for the military defence of Iceland, and that it would be best for the Icelandic government to be directly involved in the decision-making.

After a meeting with the two ambassadors, Sveinn Björnsson was under no illusion that with the imminent break-up of the Danish-Icelandic Act of Union, the two great powers fully intended to involve themselves directly in Iceland's internal affairs, which included plans for the founding of an independent Icelandic republic.

On February 9 1941, a German Heinkel carried out a bombing raid on Selfoss, and on the Kaldaðarnes airfield to the south of the town. They fired at a group of soldiers, killing one of them. The attack was fought off by anti-aircraft fire. The Heinkel flew on towards Reykjavík, where it came under fire from anti-aircraft guns on the outskirts of the city. News of the attack was broadcast on German radio, which claimed that several more aircraft were involved in the attack. The raid also drew the attention of the American media. The Washington Post considered the attack a response to the lend-lease policy currently under debate in the

US Congress, which would authorise the American government to loan weapons to the Allied forces.

In spring 1940, a Norwegian regiment was founded in Iceland, whose principal aim was to train British troops for winter warfare. Training camps were set up on the Vindheimajökull glacier, near Akureyri, and British soldiers were transported there to commence training. However, they were poorly equipped for the harsh weather, and it was rumoured that on two occasions British soldiers died of exposure.

The US army established a base in Greenland, and began a search for an appropriate location for an airfield in the south of the country. The army took over the cryolite mine at Ivigut.

There was an increase in police incidents involving both Icelanders and foreigners, in which weapons were deployed. Armed police stormed a Polish ship in Reykjavík harbour, and were met by armed crew members. Three young Icelandic girls were removed from the vessel. A mob surrounded the prison, and some demanded the women's heads be shaved.

A more serious incident occurred in March 1941 when German U-boats torpedoed and sank three Icelandic fishing vessels on their way to the British Isles. Thirty fishermen lost their lives. As a result, trawler owners refused to continue transporting shipments of fish to the British Isles. U-boat attacks were on the rise, and in late March the Germans declared that the militarised zone of the Atlantic reached as far north as the Denmark Strait. At the same time they announced an embargo on Icelandic shipping. They acknowledged that Roosevelt had declared the waters off the east coast of Iceland neutral, but claimed this was no longer valid.

That winter, British warships dropped anchor in Hvalfjörður to take on water and fuel from a tanker. The British laid a double row of mines at the mouth of the deep, inaccessible fjord. Work on the facilities there had begun, and continued until the summer of 1941, using foreign contractors and an Icelandic workforce; by that time large numbers of Icelanders were working for the occupying forces. British warships would now sail out to meet convoys

Coffins of Icelandic Seamen killed by German subs brought to Reykjavík.

coming from the west, to escort them to British ports. Within the space of twelve days, twelve ships were sunk off the south and west coasts of Iceland. Survivors were rescued by fishing boats and British warships and taken to Iceland. The loss of life was considerable, and costly shipments disappeared into the sea. On April 4 1941, ten out of the twenty-two vessels in Convoy SC 26 were sunk. Admiral Stark of the US Navy decided that further protection was needed, and deployed part of the Pacific fleet to the north Atlantic. By this time, the establishment of a naval base in Iceland was considered a matter of urgency. Roosevelt ordered the destroyer USS Niblack to sail to Iceland and scout for possible locations along the coast. The president's advisors summoned the Icelandic ambassador to a secret meeting with Cordell Hull at the White House to discuss a United States' takeover of the military defence of the island.

Around that time, Roosevelt entrusted the military council to organise dealings with the Allies, who were awaiting large shipments of weaponry from the States, after the lend lease agreement was confirmed by Congress. The military council entered negotiations with British army commanders. Under the ABC-1 agreements, provisions were made for an eventual US takeover of the military defence of Iceland. The British strengthened their air fleet in Iceland with the new Lockheed-Hudson aircraft, which were used to escort convoys. A Norwegian Squadron was formed. It received 18 new Northrop seaplanes, which were assembled in Reykjavík, and five Catalina seaplanes. The squadron was active in

Part of the first British group stationed in Hvalfjörður.

Iceland for the next two years, and during that period would lose eleven aircraft and twenty-two men, mostly at sea.

Reports were received of a sighting of the Bismarck, escorted by five battleships. At 50,000 tons, the Bismarck was the second largest vessel in the German Navy. Another large vessel, the 48,000-ton HMS Hood, was patrolling the Icelandic coast, along with four smaller battleships. On May 7 and 9 1941, Convoy OB 318 was attacked in the North Atlantic and six of its vessels were sunk. One hundred and nineteen men were rescued and taken to Reykjavík. One of the U-boats that took part in the attack was captured and towed to Hvalfjörður, but sank on the way.

Parliamentary elections in Iceland were due to be held in the early summer of 1941. However, a majority of members of parliament agreed that in light of the situation, they should be postponed for up to four years. Some members protested, and one resigned. On the eve of May 17 1941, parliament passed three resolutions: there would be no renewal of the Act of Union with Denmark due in 1943, an Icelandic republic would be founded, and elections would be held for the post of governor.

The British were building an airfield to the south of Reykjavík, and hundreds of men were employed in the construction works. On May 23 1941, the first aircraft landed on the new airfield. The previous day, a German plane had been sighted in the east, over Reyðarfjörður, before it crashed into a mountain in thick fog. A few days later a search party was sent to the wreckage and four mangled bodies were found. They were given a military burial in Reyðarfjörður, and British soldiers fired a three-volley salute. The flight was later connected with the sailing of the Bismarck and the Prinz Eugen, which were heading along the north coast of Iceland to the Denmark Strait. A British fleet went to meet them, with HMS Hood taking the lead.

Around the same time, another attack was launched on Convoy HX 126, sinking 9 of its 30 vessels. Two hundred and two men were rescued and taken to Reykjavík, but close to 200 lost their lives.

In the early hours of May 24, the British and German ships

came within firing range of one another. At 5h52, the Prinz Eugen shelled HMS Hood, causing a fire to break out on deck. Moments later, the Bismarck also opened fire, splitting HMS Hood in two. She took three minutes to go down. Out of a crew of 1,422 men, only three survived. They were taken to Reykjavík. The race was now on to pursue the German vessels and sink them. All nearby ships joined the search, and aircraft were deployed until their fuel ran out. On May 27, the Bismarck was tracked down and subjected to sustained Allied fire, until she went down at 11h01, with the loss of 2,086 lives. One hundred and fourteen men were saved.

Later that day, President Roosevelt declared a state of emergency in all forty-eight states of the union, after which he gave a radio address to the nation. He highlighted the loss of ships in previous weeks, and the enormous military significance of Iceland in the defence of North America, announcing that the US would defend itself wherever its security was threatened. The next day, Roosevelt made clear his interest in taking over the military defence of Iceland, and he informed Churchill of his intentions. Churchill's issued a response the following day welcoming the proposal. Preparations were then set in motion for the US to take over the defence of the island. Most significantly of all, Roosevelt agreed that enemy aircraft entering Iceland's airspace would be treated as such. Unbeknownst to Germany and its allies, the United States had now entered the war. Icelanders were also unaware that the defence of their country was in the process of changing hands.

On June 17 1941, parliament voted in favour of the resolutions of May 17, and Sveinn Björnsson, who was sole candidate for the position of governor, was elected. He began receiving foreign diplomats on June 21.

The following night, the mighty German army and its puppets invaded Soviet territory from the Arctic Ocean south of the Black Sea in the biggest military manoeuvre in history: Operation Barbarossa. The battlefront was 1,800 kilometres long, and the invading army consisted of three million men, attacking in V formation that was 2,500 km wide from north to south.

That same day, the first brigade of US marines left South Carolina for Argentia in Newfoundland, where a 25-vessel fleet was waiting to take them to Iceland.

On June 24, the British ambassador, Howard Smith, met with Prime Minister Hermann Jónasson, and informed him that the military defence of his country was changing hands. Aware that the Icelanders wouldn't be happy about this, British diplomats suggested the decision be presented to them as a fait accompli. However, Roosevelt was keen to have the blessing of the Icelandic government. Ambassador Smith met with the Icelandic government twice to settle the issue. Sveinn Björnsson held his first state council meeting on June 27, in which he accepted Smith's arguments. This was a sensitive issue: by agreeing to postpone parliamentary elections, parliament had effectively extended its term in power, and yet many of them believed they had no mandate. However, Jónasson was eager to seize what he saw as an opportunity: the British must agree to recognise Iceland's national sovereignty, and not to renege on it when peace treaties were drawn up at the end of the war. No one had forgotten the way in which the victors had drawn up their peace treaties after the Great War to serve their own interests, without conferring with the defeated nations and other ethnic groups. Trade relations between Iceland and Great Britain had to continue to be strengthened, even after the Americans took over the defence of the island. The great powers made their own agreements, and the Americans agreed to the British demand to retain facilities on the island for their navy and air forces. The Icelandic government knew nothing about this under-the-table deal. Frequent telegrams were relayed between the two continents before a deal was reached, and in the end a clause was added to the effect that no coloured troops would be included in the American forces posted to Iceland. On July 1 1941 the agreement was signed, and the US became the first country to recognise Iceland as an independent nation state. At the time, these agreements were treated as top-secret.

On July 4, it was announced in a Berlin radio report and a United Press newsflash, quoting Senator Burton Wheeler as the source, that the United States was to take over the military defence of Iceland. The Icelandic government denied any knowledge of this.

Task force 19 was the name of the operation comprising 25 vessels, which set sail from Argentia on July 1. One day earlier, other ships left for Ivigut in Greenland, where the plan was to establish an army base, Bluie 1, as well as an airfield. On July 3, four Catalina seaplanes set off to Iceland, but one crashed into the sea. The 25- vessel convoy arrived in Reykjavík on July 7. That same evening, men and military equipment were moved onto land. The troops numbered approximately 4,000 and were transported to stations just outside Reykjavík. In contrast to the British, who set up their Nissen huts on vacant lots inside the city, the Americans preferred to install their barracks outside the city limits. That evening, the BBC broadcast news of the agreement, and the Icelandic prime minister gave a radio address to the nation to explain the changes to Iceland's defence. The matter was raised in parliament on the evening of July 9, and discussions went on into the night. The agreement was passed by a majority ballot with only a few votes against.

The Yanks arrive: USS Republic seen in the mist from USS Tuscaloosa.

Arrival in Reykjavík. The helmets were from the Great War and were soon replaced with more identifiable ones.

With the arrival of the American army, there were close to 35,000 foreign men on the island, more than a quarter of the local population. One Member of Parliament, who abstained from the vote on July 9, was Vilmundur Jónsson, Director of Public Health. He considered he had no mandate. Two days later, he sent a letter to the Minister of Justice, making clear his concerns about relations between Icelandic womenfolk and foreign soldiers.

In the latter part of 1940, the Minister of Justice had enlisted a woman into the Reykjavík police force to deal with female issues in particular – something the women's movement had long been demanding. Among the recruits was a respected nurse, who had already spoken to the government about her concerns regarding relationships between local Icelandic women and British, Canadian and Norwegian soldiers. The Minister of Justice and the Chief of Police entrusted her to investigate these relationships. She made use of existing police data, and hired additional researchers to carry out a comprehensive study of 800 individuals from 200 households, which included detailed information on 141 underage girls, and close to 350 adult females. She presented the results to the authorities, including the Director of Public Health, Vilmundur Jónsson, who wrote to the Minister of Justice about his concerns over the immoral relations which young girls and adult women maintained with members of the armed forces.

The minister set up a commission to which he appointed a doctor, a psychologist and a priest. So far, the enquiry had remained confidential, but by the end of August, newspapers had published the report's conclusions, and paperboys on street corners could be heard shouting: "500 whores in the port of Reykjavík". Researchers found that a group of underage girls were engaging in illicit sexual relations with soldiers, and a large group of women "of low morals" who were the principal carers of some 300 children. The Reykjavík Chief of Police considered the problem far more widespread than the report suggested. Some journalists questioned the motives of the research, and the government's right to probe so comprehensively into people's personal lives. A handful of men pointed out that women weren't alone in being servile to the army, and that some Icelandic men were too. A serious proposal was mooted that brothels catering exclusively to the armed forces be established.

Then, and in the years that followed, the debate over the propriety of the army's relations with Icelandic women would be tainted by patriotism, and puritanism. The idea that many young girls were simply seeking the soldiers' friendship and were taken advantage of has long since been rejected. The British military authorities made their own detailed observations on the report and its findings, and considered the problem to have been exaggerated: soldiers were forbidden from receiving guests at their barracks, and soldiers engaging in sexual relations with minors risked court martial. At the end of September 1941, strict laws were put in place aimed at curtailing relations between the occupying forces and the local female population: women under the age of eighteen were prohibited from associating with soldiers, it was advised that children from problem families should be taken into care, and three refuges would be set up to house fallen women. A special tribunal was established to judge young delinquents of both sexes.

Eye to eye in Aðalstræti. A soldier with his rifle talking to a woman on a street in Reykjavík.

The US armed forces were quick to step up their activities after they arrived in July 1941. In August, Mariner and Catalina seaplanes, and Warhawk fighter planes arrived on the island, along with gigantic troop carriers. All their foodstuffs were imported: this included products that were scarce or had never been seen before. New kinds of music could be heard emanating from their ships' holds. While the first British troops to arrive were equipped with weapons and uniforms dating back to the Great War, the Americans were better dressed, in new uniforms with different shaped helmets. Everything moved at a faster pace: freight ships equipped with cranes took days instead of weeks to unload their cargoes. The arrival of the US Army heralded a new age in Europe: this was the American era.

Collaboration between the United States and Great Britain was further strengthened when Roosevelt and Churchill met at Placentia Bay on August 9–12. Under discussion were eight sections of the Atlantic Charter, and in the following month 26 countries undersigned the principles of the agreement. The charter affirmed that neither Great Britain nor the United States would engage in land grabbing, that they would treat all other nations equally, respect their right to freedom, to self-determination, and to engage in free trade. This charter established British and American cooperation.

USS Almaack unloading in Reykjavik on August 6 1941.

The first day of the meeting in Argentia: from left Franklin D. Roosevelt Jr., Winston Churchill, President Roosevelt and his older son, Elliot.

Churchill leaving Reykjavík for inspection of the troops in Hvalfjörður.

Following the meeting in Placentia Bay, Churchill sailed to Iceland, where he visited some army bases, met with the governor and the prime minister, had lunch in Höfði, and attended a military parade. Churchill had promised assistance to Stalin in his fight against the superior power of the German Army, and the first convoy to sail into Hvalfjörður carrying military equipment was destined for Arkhangelsk. This was the beginning of many transports via Hvalfjörður both to Arkhangelsk and to Murmansk in the years to come.

Curtiss P-40C Warhawk from the 33rd US squadron coming in from Kaldaðar-nes-airport hit a tractor while landing in Reykjavik Airport. The driver jumped out of his seat and the pilot got out in time. He was immediately put in another plane and ordered to take off to overwin the shock of the crash.

The deck of U-570 by the USS Vulcan in Hvalfjörður, where the submarine was repaired. U-570 was on his maiden-voyage in the open seas when a Hudson from Kaldaðarnes sighted the sub on August 24.

At the end of August 1941, British fighter planes from Kaldaðarnes disabled a German U-boat. The inexperienced crew surrendered and was placed under arrest. The U-boat was towed into land on the south coast of Iceland. A British crew then took charge of it, and towed it to Hvalfjörður, where it was cleaned and searched before being sailed to the British Isles. The crew was detained in a British POW camp, where the U-boat commanders were branded cowards by their fellow German prisoners. Both commanders were placed in isolation for their own safety.

German U-boats inflicted huge losses. In the first week of September, three trawlers transporting fish to the British Isles were sunk. A group of U-boats, a so-called "wolfpack", sustained a 10-day attack on Convoy SC 42 off the coast of Greenland. Sixteen ships were sunk and four damaged with a loss of 270 lives. One hundred and seven men were rescued from the sea and taken to Reykjavík. Two of the attacking U-boats were destroyed, as by that time better-equipped aircraft were stationed in Iceland for patrol and bombing excursions.

On September 5, a German U-boat fired at the American battleship USS Greer. This was the first attack on an American vessel

The third phase of transport of US troops – Indigo III – moved 5,000 soldiers from Argentia to Reykjavík on September 5 1941.

since the outbreak of hostilities. The USS Greer managed to get to Reykjavík a few days later. Later the same day, a 16-vessel convoy set sail for Iceland carrying 5,000 troops and provisions. It arrived ten days later.

On September 11 1941, Roosevelt gave an address to the nation. He mentioned the attack on USS Greer, and the other convoy vessels en route to Iceland. He held consultations with the Russian ambassador and some of his own high-ranking officials. The attack on USS Greer infuriated the Americans, and in his condemnation, Roosevelt declared: "... Let this warning be clear. From now on, if German or Italian vessels of war enter the waters, the protection of which is necessary for American defence, they do so at their own peril." It was instantly dubbed the "shoot first" order. On September 15 Convoy HX 150 sailed from Halifax with 41 vessels under the protection of the US Navy.

The damage on USS Kearney.

The US Navy had its work cut out: from September through to October, 656 merchant ships sailed east in 11 convoys escorted by approximately 200 ships. Convoy SC 48 sailed into a storm, and the convoy was broken up. On October 15, three vessels were sunk, and two US destroyers, USS Greer and USS Kearney came to assist. A further five vessels were sunk on October 17, with a loss of 253 lives. Eighty-one men were rescued and taken to Reykjavík. Then, during a dawn attack on USS Kearney, 11 men were killed and 22 wounded, eight of them seriously. Blood supplies were flown in from Reykjavík, and USS Greer towed the damaged vessel to Hvalfjörður. The following day, a British destroyer was sunk, 88 men were saved and 56 lost, 11 of them trying to escape in lifeboats.

The attack on USS Kearney was momentous. This was the first time Americans lives had been lost during a German attack, and before long a US warship was sunk off the coast of Iceland. The destroyer USS Reuben James was torpedoed on October 31, and sank immediately. Forty-four men survived and 116 were lost.

Icelandic diplomats arrived from Washington bearing fresh trade agreements from the United States. The Americans guaranteed all British obligations, goods exported to the British market would be paid for in US dollars, and Icelandic importers were guaranteed goods from America and the vessels in which to transport them. In addition, assurances were given that levies on Icelandic exports would be reconsidered. The members of the deputation looked after their own personal interests: one bought a refrigerator, another a car, and two became concessionaries of the Coca Cola company in Iceland. The journey home was a long one; the crew was made up of inexperienced oil workers from Oklahoma, and the ship had to be turned around when the engines failed during a severe storm. They didn't reach port until Christmas. It was later disclosed in the White Falcon, the US Army's journal, that in addition to the trade deal, Iceland would be loaned 25 million dollars.

Have a Coca-Cola = Come, be blessed and be happy

...or how to break the ice in Iceland

Coca Cola had been in great demand in Iceland in the autumn of 1941, but by the end of the year a large plant started mixing icelandic water with the syrup imported in barrels from the US.

Convoys PQ and QP, which sailed back and forth to Murmansk, set the pace for maritime transports. Supplies were stockpiled in Hvalfjörður. The convoys transported military equipment to the Red Army, and were forced to navigate as far north as possible due to the risk of German raids from airfields in northern Norway. These journeys were perilous, because ships became heavily iced, and ocean temperatures were impossible to survive, in case of any mishaps.

*HMS Sheffield sailing with a convoy in
December 1941 on the way to Murmansk.*

The air fleet in Iceland was expanded, and yet few pilots had experience in flying in that kind of climate, and many lives were lost as aircraft went down, or crashed into mountains in bad weather. The Icelandic fishing fleet also suffered setbacks, both due to the war, and the forces of nature: the trawler Sviði sank off the Westfjords on December 2 with the loss of 25 men.

On December 7 1941, the Japanese launched an air attack on the American naval base, Pearl Harbour, Hawaii. They sank several ships, and the base suffered extensive damage. One of them was USS Arizona with a loss of 1,177 crewmen, among them Howard Helgi, the son of Þrúður Þorláksson from Akranes. The generation of Icelanders that moved to the States and Canada around the turn of the century, one fifth of Icelanders at the time, started to feel the cost of war. The United States, Canada and Great Britain declared war on Japan, and four days later, Hitler and Mussolini declared war on the United States.

At the end of 1941, the political situation in Iceland heated up. The worker's movement had called a strike to demand wage increases in a country plagued by inflation. Parliament was rife with partisan politics, and the formation of a government looked unlikely after the Social Democrats resigned from the coalition as a result of its refusal to act on rising price.

In December 1941, weekly shipments of provisions and troops commenced between Iceland and the British Isles. These were identified by the letters RU and UR, and continued until the spring of 1945.

With the arrival of winter, troops undertook long treks through the snow as part of their training. In January 1942 sixty soldiers from the King's Own Yorkshire Light Infantry were sent off on a mountain hike in the east of Iceland. They were caught in a torrential downpour, followed by freezing temperatures and a snowstorm. Close to exhaustion, one of them made it to Vesturhús farm, where he managed to raise the alarm. Two young brothers, one aged 12, went out in the storm to search for the beleaguered men. At daybreak, the older brother went out again, accompanied by some of the British soldiers who had recovered their strength, and by evening they had managed to bring back alive to the farm a total of 48 men. Eight died of exposure, and two others who got separated managed to reach a populated area. It was no wonder that their American fellow soldiers referred to the country as "a frozen hell".

On January 29 1942, while patrolling the Icelandic coast close to Reykjavík, a newly built coastguard cutter, the USCGC Alexander Hamilton went to assist a supply ship with engine trouble. The Alexander Hamilton had a crew of 221 men, most of them young, raw recruits. Shortly after midday, a U-boat fired four torpedoes at the three vessels escorting the supply ship. One of them hit the boiler room of the coastguard cutter, which filled with scalding water and steam. Four men died in the explosion, five others were trapped, and three lifeboats broke away from the davit arms. The ship began to sink slowly. Six other vessels ventured through heavy seas to assist them. Three fishing boats that were on their way back to land rescued 83 men; two sailed for Reykjavík and the third sailed to where the nearest doctor was located, in Keflavík. The USS Gwin rescued 101 other crew members. The wounded men had suffered severe burns, and six of them died. A total of twenty lives were lost in the attack.

*The arrival of frost and snow was a shock for the troops,
whose clothing wasn't designed for the cold Icelandic winters.
An iced-up truck sits sheltered from the weather.*

USCGC Alexander Hamilton sinking.

At the beginning of the occupation, the British considered that an invading army would most likely land to the north, in the broad, deep bay of Húnaflói. Army bases were set up in Hrútafjörður, and the summer of 1940 saw the arrival of troops recently evacuated from Dunkirk. The men were emotional and traumatised. Men and goods were put on to barges via a ropeway and taken ashore. On February 13, 24 soldiers in full military gear crossed the fjord in a barge. However, the vessel was overloaded and capsized. Two local men managed to get a small boat out to them and rescued six of the soldiers, but they couldn't take on any more without overloading their own boat, and many others were drowned in desperate circumstances. The army kept quiet about the incident, but the people who lived in Hrútafjörður never forgot it, and the bodies never washed up.

Sixty American nurses arrive in Reykjavík aboard the SS Borinquin on March 3 1942. They were deployed at a hospital near Helgafell in Mosfellssveit. In some instances, fully-fledged hospitals were built to serve the US forces. That same day 5,200 fresh recruits and army personnel also arrived.

The soldiers had few ways of amusing themselves until the summer of 1942, when film screenings and other forms of entertainment were arranged for the benefit of the American troops. Most went to the cinema, and sales of tickets in Reykjavík cinemas jumped from 312,000 in 1939 to 928,000 in 1942. Up until it was prohibited in autumn 1940, soldiers would attend public screenings armed.

In the winter of 1942 there was a rise in cases of aggressive and violent behaviour on the part of US troops, often during patrols, and without reasonable cause. In March, a man was killed at an observation post, a British soldier sodomised a young boy, and on one occasion shots were fired; American soldiers seemed more trigger-happy than their British predecessors.

The needs of the occupying forces led to a significant shortage of labour. The Icelandic government tried unsuccessfully to set a limit on how many people the army could hire. Forty small vessels were employed to run errands up and down the coastline, and when spring arrived, there was a shortage of men both in the fisheries and in agriculture. Reykjavík's biggest hotel was forced to close due to a lack of available staff.

On Sunday, March 15 1942 local elections took place all over the country. The inhabitants of Reykjavík were alarmed when a loud bang was heard coming from the airfield, and a plume of smoke rose into the air: a fully-loaded Lancaster bomber with a crew of seven had crashed into the munitions dump on take off, causing a huge explosion. All the crew were killed, but no one on the airfield was hurt.

PQ13

Convoy QP 9 left Murmansk on March 21 1942. It was made up of 18 ships and a 32-vessel escort. HMS Kenya was loaded with 10 tons of gold, and the other ships carried cargoes of timber and crude metals. The entire fleet reached its destination. A minesweeper sailed into and sank a German U-boat. Forty-five of the crew were drowned.

A sister convoy of 18 ships, the PQ 13, sailed from Loch Ewe on March 10. The convoy was dispersed due to bad weather, which increased the risk of U-boat attacks. The lead ship was the 5,086 ton steam merchant vessel, Induna, carrying a 2,700 ton cargo of barbed wire, aircraft fuel and army vehicles. The crew came from various different countries, and included an eighteen-year-old Icelander. Another Icelandic youth was aboard SS Ballot. On March 18, the convoy regrouped, but then turned back because of U-boat sightings in the area. A number of other escort ships joined the convoy, and on March 20, they set sail once more. Bad weather struck again on March 23, and the boats became heavily iced. The convoy was scattered, and one escort ship was lost in the storm. The young Icelander's vessel joined other ships from the convoy, but on March 28, a German seaplane spotted them and opened fire. The anti-aircraft guns on the cruiser HMS Trinidad were frozen solid, and had to be dismantled and greased. SS Ballot suffered engine failure, and was cast adrift. A number of her crew decamped to a whaling boat, HMS Silja. However, once the engines on SS Ballot were repaired, the captain decided to sail on alone to Murmansk. His ship reached port on March 30.

SS Raceland didn't fare as well. She was carrying aircraft parts, tanks, trucks, ammunition, and 2,700 tons of raw metals when she sank. The crew escaped onto four lifeboats, two of which went missing during the night. As well as fighter planes, the Germans deployed fast-moving destroyers, and when SS Empire Ranger went down, one them rescued her crew. Five ships went to assist SS Silja, which had run out of fuel near the ice shelf. The Induna towed her, but during the night the towrope broke, and the Silja vanished into the darkness. A search was made during daylight, but she was never found.

Another group of ships from the convoy were being escorted by HMS Eclipse. Both HMS Trinidad and HMS Fury had been separated from the convoy, and two Soviet destroyers joined the search for other vessels from the convoy. The German destroyers caught up with HMS Trinidad, and the two ships engaged in combat. A direct hit left a large hole in the Trinidad, and one of the destroyers lost her prow. One of HMS Trinidad's torpedoes turned full circle and hit her. A fire broke out on board, and it was decided she should steam ahead to Murmansk. Still ablaze, HMS Trinidad reached the harbour in the early hours of March 30.

HMS Eclipse took on the German destroyer Z-26 and sank her. Another vessel went to the aid of the Z-26, and rescued 250 men. Seventy others lost their lives. Later that day German U-boats approached four ships close to the ice shelf. SS Effingham was sunk. The crew escaped into two lifeboats, and were eventually picked up. In one of the boats ten men were found alive and seven dead, and in the other 19 men were found alive alongside four frozen bodies.

A torpedo struck SS Induna's hold. She was carrying aircraft fuel, and a raging fire enveloped the sinking ship. Two lifeboats got away, leaving twenty-five men on board. The lifeboats had a capacity of 25, but one was carrying 34 men, and the other only nine. By the following day, half the men in the overloaded boat were dead, while all those on the other survived. The young Icelander was in the engine room when the ship went down. Four days earlier his son had been born. His fellow countryman on the Ballot made it home to his wife and young child.

The lifeboats from SS Raceland ran aground. Thirteen men escaped with their lives and 20 died of exposure.

The ships that reached Murmansk found themselves immediately caught up in a German air attack, and two were sunk in the harbour. Women transferred the cargo to freight trains, and the ordinary seamen weren't allowed to disembark, although the officers visited a brothel known as "Churchill Hotel" where women were allegedly kept as sex slaves.

One year after the ABC-1 agreement between Great Britain and the United States, the majority of British troops had been posted outside Iceland, although a number of them remained there until the end of the war. On the night of April 18 1942, three large passenger ships transporting reinforcements to Iceland sailed into Reykjavík harbour. The 5th Division of Light Infantry disembarked, bringing the total of US troops on the island to 26,000, a far greater number than at any time during the British occupation. Four days later, the same three ships transported most of the remaining British soldiers to Gourock, in Scotland. In Europe and America, it was reported in the media that the United States had taken over the command of military operations in Iceland.

Major General Charles H. Bonesteel, who had in charge of US field forces since the autumn, was now in command. Protocol was tightened up: marriages between soldiers and Icelandic women were banned, the use of public transport by soldiers was limited, and a proper waste disposal system was installed. They hired a man who had worked as an interpreter and mediator for the British Army, a known Icelandic socialist, to organise the waste disposal at the US barracks outside Reykjavík. He selected likeminded comrades, with experience of trade union struggles, to assist him. The Americans discarded a lot of food, such as damaged tinned goods, and bruised fresh fruit. For many the locals it was a godsend to able to salvage this produce, which would otherwise have been disposed of by the supply personnel. In the summer of 1942, the British barracks were cleared out, and a lot of furniture, gadgets and provisions were discarded. The inhabitants of Reykjavík would go to the rubbish tips, and take away anything that was still usable.

American marines on Bankastræti. Despite the clause in the agreement the previous summer regarding US military defence of the island, men of colour from various ethnic backgrounds were amongst the troops.

Catalina seaplane came under attack from friendly fire 300 miles out to sea, but managed to reach land on one engine. Of the five-man crew, one was badly injured, one suffered from shock, and the other three were unharmed. Their lifeboat can be seen close to the group of men on the beach.

Two years into the occupation, a bomber aircraft crashed on the runway at Reykjavík airfield, after making a ten-hour flight from Gander in Newfoundland. Three crewmembers were on board. One of the aircraft's wings clipped a house close to the airfield, and the plane turned over. The inhabitants of the building managed to escape, and the emergency services arrived at the scene, but an oil tanker parked nearby burst into flames. Two of the airmen managed to escape the wreckage, but one remained trapped in his seat and was put out of his misery with a bullet to the head. One of the people who lived in the building died a month later, and the cause of death was attributed to the air crash. The incident was not reported in the daily newspapers. It wasn't uncommon for aircraft to crash-land outside the perimeter fence of an airfield and burst into flames. First responders at the scene would administer the death blow to anyone trapped in the burning wreckage.

ESPIONAGE IN ICELAND

Ib Riis Árnason, one of the Britain's foremost double agents in Iceland. COBWEB was his MI6 secret codename, while the German naval intelligence services knew him as EDDA. This photograph was taken after the war, and he is dressed in the uniform of a chief mate, which the British insisted he wear in Reykjavík.

The Americans hunted down and destroyed German weather ships and their radio transmitters in Greenland. The German Naval Intelligence Service, the Abwehr, planned to set up a network of spies in Iceland to send weather reports to Germany via secret transmitters. Towards the end of 1941, they approached an out-of-work radio operator, Ib Árnason, in Copenhagen. He attended a meeting at the Hotel Cosmopolite, the headquarters of the Abwehrsteile Dänemark, where he met with the Germans. Ib was recruited to travel to Iceland as a spy. He was trained in Hamburg, and was provided with a secret code name, EDDA, a codebook, a radio transmitter and 3,000 US dollars. As a safety measure, he informed his parents and sister about his work, having decided to give himself up to the Icelandic authorities as soon as he arrived in the country. On March 22 1942 he was taken by U-boat U-252 to Finnafjörður, in north-east Iceland. The U-boat then continued along the north coast. On April 9, it came within range of a Norwegian merchant vessel off the Westfjords, and sank it. Twenty-six men were killed. Five days later, the U-boat was sunk in the Bay of Biscay with the loss of 44 men.

Ib made his presence known at the first place he came to, which was a farm called Fell. The following day he gained access to a telephone, and called the county sheriff in Seyðisfjörður. A few days later, the British came to pick him up, and put him on a coastguard ship to Reykjavík. Ib was open and helpful during an interview with the British intelligence services. He provided a written account of the set-up at Hotel Cosmopolite, his experiences in Copenhagen and Hamburg, and of the U-boat that took him to Iceland, furnishing them every detail he could to try to persuade them that they could trust him. Afterwards, he was flown back to Finnafjörður to pick up the things he had left there. The day after, he was instructed to make his location known via radio transmitter, and was then put on a flight back to London. There he was held in solitary confinement and underwent further interrogations. He then spent a few days in a comfortable apartment in London, and was finally put on a flight to Reykjavík, where he was summoned to an interview, and told that he was now an MI6 double agent. His job was to send bogus, encoded messages to Germany at specific hours every weekday.

The site of the proposed airfield, where Keflavík International Airport is now located. Men are still living in tents and building roads.

Already by autumn 1941, the Americans had realised that the airfields built by the British in 1940 weren't equipped to receive the heavy cargo planes scheduled to arrive. The runways at the Reykjavík and Kaldaðarnes airfields, and the smaller ones scattered about the country, weren't long enough for four-engine aircraft to land safely. In November 1941, using studies carried out by the British, the military council drew up plans for an airfield on the Reykjanes peninsula. The moraine-covered plain on Rosmhvalanes was considered eligible. Four small harbours were located nearby, there was plenty of local material for the substrate, and the contour lines were favourable. The military council gave the project a green light, and stumped up 10 million dollars for its implementation. The space required to build the airfield covered an area 248 square kilometres, almost half of which belonged to ten farming families. Negotiations were started with the new government lead by Ólafur Thors. An agreement was reached on May 18 1942, after which public access to the area was restricted.

On Whitsun 1942, a US soldier on patrol shot and killed a ten-year-old boy he had seen messing around with a vehicle parked near a Nissen hut in the centre of Reykjavík. The soldier was given a mental health assessment and declared unfit to stand trial.

At the end of May 1942, Soviet Prime Minister and Foreign Minister Molotov stopped off in Reykjavík on his way to the United States. Other Soviet diplomats reportedly arrived in Reykjavík around the same time.

Large transports of military equipment were expected via new routes. Since the summer of 1940, aircraft from France and Great Britain had to be shipped over, because none were equipped to travel the long distances over the ocean, even with extra fuel tanks. In the autumn of 1940, a company of British and Canadian professional pilots started to fly bigger aircraft to Belfast via Gander. The following summer, new routes to Iceland were considered via Greenland. However, those routes were hazardous, and when autumn came flights ceased. By then, over 600 aircraft had flown across the ocean.

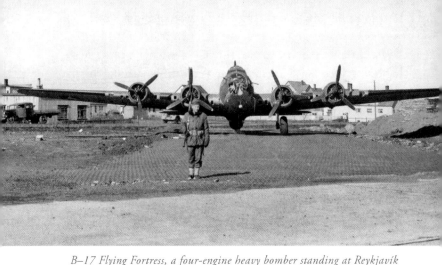

B–17 Flying Fortress, a four-engine heavy bomber standing at Reykjavík airfield. They would herald the beginning of a fresh chapter in the war.

Army Air Transport Command (AATC) was founded in June 1942, and oversaw all US transportations. That year, under the auspices of the AATC, 920 aircraft flew across the ocean, 600 of them via Reykjavík. Eight hundred and eighty-two arrived at their final destinations, 9 were lost, and 29 damaged. At the same time, the British flew 791 aircraft across the ocean, 123 of which took the perilous northern route. Twenty of them were lost. Thus, in the summer of 1942, a steady stream of aircraft passed through Reykjavík airfield en route to the British Isles, where they were eagerly awaited.

Convoy PQ 17 left Hvalfjörður with 35 merchant vessels carrying a valuable cargo: 297 aircraft, 594 tanks, 4,246 trucks and gun carriages, as well as 156,000 tons of military equipment and supplies worth 700 million US dollars. Twelve escort ships sailed alongside the convoy, as well as two submarines, and eight more escort vessels would join them off the north east coast of Iceland. Four Icelandic youths were on board the lead ship, SS Ironclad, the crew of which was made up of ex-criminals and murderers serving out their sentences in the navy. Two other Icelanders, whose identities are unknown, were on another vessel, SS Troubadour.

The airfields in northern Norway were shrouded in fog, delaying take off for the German fighter aircraft. The German battleship Tirpitz and the cruiser Admiral Hipper were sailing through the Norwegian skerries towards the open ocean. The British fleet received intelligence about a large German taskforce heading out to sea. The cruiser, Admiral Scheer, joined the taskforce. On the morning of July 4, a Heinkel bomber opened fire on the lead vessel, a 7,000-ton Liberty ship, which sank. By approximately 15h00, a large squadron of aircraft were circling the convoy, and other fighter planes were on their way. When the planes came within firing range, the destroyer, USS Wainwright, steered round and trained all her guns on the attacking squadron. In the resulting crossfire, eight German aircraft were shot down, by which time two vessels in the convoy were sinking.

That evening, Admiral of the Fleet Sir Dudley Pound, mistakenly believing that the German ships were moving to intercept, ordered Convoy PQ 17 to scatter. The convoy divided into two sections, with 19 vessels in one and 13 in the other. The captain of the Ironclad sailed his ship towards the ice shelf, and three others followed. One was carrying gallons of white paint in her hold, and the crew was ordered to paint the ships white. The four vessels remained hidden for forty-eight hours.

On July 5, six ships came under fire and were sunk. Thirty-eight men were lost, and 28 others taken prisoner on board German vessels or U-boats. Among them was a man called Théodor Kristján from the west of Iceland. A British ship and a German seaplane quickly rescued 104 shipwrecked sailors, while four lifeboats with 57 men on board made for land. By the time they reached the shore, 45 were alive and 12 were dead.

Later that day, the attacks resumed and a further five ships were sunk. On July 6, two ships were sunk, on July 7, four ships went down and another on July 8. Of the original 34 vessels in the convoy, the Germans sank 24. Seventy-seven crewmembers from the convoy were taken prisoner by the Germans, all of whom were detained in POW camps in Norway, where they remained until the end of the war. Of the survivors who reached Murmansk, many were in bad shape; 50 of the 129 men transported by one ship were unable to walk.

The British ploy to make the Germans believe that a large convoy was travelling further south had apparently worked, and it was Ib Riis who transmitted the message from Iceland.

Sir Dudley Pound's fears that the German battleships had been searching for Convoy PQ 17 were groundless. They had been sent in search of a non-existent convoy.

Even so, Convoy PQ 17 remains the biggest maritime disaster in the history of Russian Artic convoys, of which there were many.

CONVOY QP13 – THE BIGGEST MARITIME ACCIDENT OFF THE ICELANDIC COAST

On June 26 1942, a convoy of 35 merchant ships with a seven-vessel escort left Murmansk for Hvalfjörður. Nine of the ships were carrying passengers, diplomats travelling to Washington and London, and approximately 120 sailors rescued from other convoys. German aircraft located the convoy on the fifth day, but thick fog enabled the ships to continue unharmed.

Somewhere off the coast of Langanes, the convoy divided; one section headed straight for Scotland, while 19 other vessels sailed north, escorted by minesweepers HMS Niger and HMS Hussar, the corvette Roselys, and two armed trawlers. The weather was bad, and visibility poor. They were heading for a gap in the North Sea Mine Barrage, unaware that one month earlier a fresh batch of mines had been laid. When the Niger thought she sighted Hornbjarg, the North Western Cape of Iceland, she changed course. Six other vessels, also mislead by what subsequently proved to be an iceberg, followed the Niger into the barrage.

Seconds later, HMS Niger detonated a mine, capsized and sank with a crew of 80 men on board, together with 39 survivors from HMS Edinburgh, who had already been shipwrecked and were on their way home.

The next ship to hit a mine was the merchant vessel Hybert, with a crew of 54, together with 26 sailors who had been rescued six weeks earlier. The ship sank slowly, and all the men managed to escape onto lifeboats.

Then it was the turn of the Heffron. Of the 76 men on board several had been rescued from convoys PQ 15 and 16. All 76 escaped with their lives.

A mine then exploded close to the Massmar. Three lifeboats were lowered, one capsized instantly, and another was dragged down in the ship's wake with 60 men on board. One man in the last boat got away with his life.

Chaos reigned amid the towering waves. Minesweepers let off depth charges, panic-stricken men shot into the darkness and escort ships searched frantically for lifeboats.

The next vessel to hit a mine was the Soviet Rodina, a passenger ship carrying civilian men, women and children. Thirty-nine were killed and 16 rescued. Then, the Liberty ship, John Randolph blew up, and broke in two. The bow of the ship stayed afloat. Fifty-five people were rescued and five lost their lives.

The last ship to hit a mine was the freighter, Exterminator, which stayed afloat despite suffering severe damage.

Reports of the death toll that night differ. It is estimated that approximately 250 people died and the same number survived. The crew of the French corvette, Roselys, showed great bravery, leading a six-hour search and rescuing 179 people. Nearby vessels were sent to the site of the catastrophe, including a battleship, and an Icelandic trawler. The noise of the exploding mines reached as far as Aðalvík in Hornstrandir. A fishing boat sailed from there and recovered dead bodies from the sea. All summer long, bodies were found washed up on Hornstrandir. The British ban on recovering bodies went against the Icelandic custom.

Part of the convoy sailed into Ísafjarðardjúp, while the Roselys and one of the trawlers took survivors to Reykjavík, where thirty were hospitalised.

Injured merchant seamen being taken off the Roselys, in Reykjavík. In the left-hand corner are two young seamen; the dark-skinned one is tied to a stretcher.

Shipwrecked men waiting for a lift to Camp Caledonia, where they were usually held. The men on the merchant convoys came from many different countries.

The fate of Convoy QP 13, which caused the biggest loss of life of any maritime accident in Icelandic history, was kept a secret. An enquiry blamed the disaster on an insufficient dissemination of information, and the convoy commander's lack of knowledge of the area. The incident led to a radio beacon being installed on Straumnes. On July 12, an American troop carrier took 173 survivors of the convoy to Britain.

The leader of the Free French Forces, General de Gaulle, gave the crew of the Roselys a special commendation for bravery.

In August 1942, 2,333 magnetic mines were laid at depths of eight to nine metres along a 38 nautical mile stretch off the north east coast of Iceland. This was in addition to a similar number laid the previous June, in the area where Convoy QP 13's fate was decided.

On July 26 1942, General George Marshall, Commander in Chief of the US fleet Ernest J. King, and Secretary of State Harry Hopkins arrived with their entourages in Iceland. That evening, members of the Icelandic government met with the American visitors over dinner. Governor Sveinn Björnsson and Hopkins were seated together and got along famously. As the evening drew on, Hopkins took Sveinn aside. He relayed to him Roosevelt's concerns about the Icelandic government's plans to found a republic, and confided that he had been sent there to put a temporary halt to the plans. Sveinn then ushered Hopkins over to another dinner guest, the prime minister Ólafur Thors, to whom Hopkins relayed the same story. Sveinn recorded the conversation in a memo the following day. The main election promise of Ólafur Thors's party was now in disarray. On July 31, the US administration sent a letter to the Icelandic government, requesting they postpone plans to found a republic. This was, largely speaking, the only occasion on which the US had meddled in Iceland's internal affairs, and Thors had little choice but to accept.

An increasing number of visits by German aircraft set the tone for the month. On August 2, a Condor aircraft launched an attack on a British observation post in Hornafjörður, southeast Iceland, using bombs and machine guns. This was the first bomb dropped on the occupying forces in Iceland. More Condors arrived on

Aerial photograph of Reykjavík August 18 1942, taken by a Junkers JU 88 photographic reconnaissance aircraft that was subsequently repelled by anti-aircraft fire and fighter planes. The Germans carried out further flights over Iceland on August 23 and 24. The ship with a long smoke plume is the troop ship Queen of Bermuda weighing 22,575 tons, one of many ship that transported 6,000 soldiers to Iceland in August.

August 4 and 5. One was pursued and shot down over the sea, with a loss of six airmen. This was also the first time since the outbreak of hostilities that the US Army had shot down a German aircraft.

Canadian and British Special Forces launched a raid on Dieppe, on the north coast of France, and were almost wiped out. Among them was a young Icelandic boy living in Canada. There were several men of Icelandic origin in the Canadian Army, which had joined the war early on, as well as in the US Army. Some of them had been born in Iceland, although at the start of the war, approximately a fifth of the Icelandic population was living in North America. One casualty list estimates that over 2,000 soldiers in the Canadian and US armed forces who lost their lives in WWII were of Icelandic origin.

Submariners from the German submarine U-175 on the deck of HMS Spencer April 17 1943. Crew members of enemy U-boats were stripped and kept on deck if captured to ensure they did not show any resistense.

On August 20 1942, the Skaftfellingur, a motorboat from the Westmann Islands, was on its way to the British Isles with a cargo of iced fish, when it sailed past a half-submerged German U-boat. Some of the men were up on the conning tower waving a red flag. The U-464's maiden voyage had ended 200 miles south of Hornafjörður after it came under an attack from a Catalina seaplane, and the vessel was sinking with 54 men on board. The motorboat was equipped with a machine gun and a rifle, and the captain decided to try to rescue the submariners. They were told to jump into the sea, and were then hoisted onto the motorboat one by one, frisked for weapons, and ordered to sit down. During the hour or more it took to carry out the rescue mission, the U-boat sank. Soon afterwards, a British destroyer appeared, and took the German submariners on board. They were ordered to undress on deck in heavy seas, where they hunkered down wrapped in blankets. The captain of the Skaftfellingur was ordered to return to Reykjavík, but he refused, and sailed on with his six-man crew to Liverpool. When they arrived, they were interrogated, and a thorough search of the ship was carried out. All were impressed by the captain's brave exploit. Fifty-two of the U-boat's crew were saved, and two died in the attack. British naval records state that 21 of the U-boat's crew were under the age of nineteen.

In September 1942, the first Consolidated B-24 Liberators, four-engine long-range bomber and reconnaissance aircraft, arrived in Iceland under the auspices of the 120 Squadron of the RAF. The aircraft were well equipped, and before the end of the war would sink 15 German U-boats. By the end of 1941, the air squadron in Kaldaðarnes had lost eight men, one in an emergency crash landing and another at sea. During reconnaissance flights, the squadron had occasionally exchanged fire with German aircraft. By the end of 1942 the toll was 15 aircraft and 25 men.

At the beginning of September 1942, a fleet of ships was anchored off Seyðisfjörður, on the east coast of Iceland, where the largest convoy yet was preparing to set sail. The aircraft carrier HMS Avenger and twelve other vessels would escort Convoy PQ 18. Eight hundred US troops had recently arrived in the town, and British troops were moving out. Two German Condor aircraft appeared close to the mouth of the fjord, and one of them dropped two bombs. They fell where some children were playing, injuring a young boy, who lost his leg. The craters measured approximately two metres deep and twelve metres wide. Apart from a lot of shattered windows, the surrounding buildings escaped serious damage. The following day, four more aircraft flew over the town and dropped more shells, which didn't cause

Young people at Seyðisfjörður in one crater after the air raid.

any damage. A few days later, German aircraft made further sorties along the east coasts, firing at villages and boats.

When Convoy PQ 18 set sail from Hvalfjörður on September 7 1942, it was made up of 43 ships, and an escort of 12 vessels and two submarines. The following day, eight more ships from Seyðisfjörður joined the escort, which in the end numbered 38 vessels. On September 13, sixty-three German aircraft opened fire on the convoy, sinking eight ships in the space of thirteen minutes. By the time the attack ended, thirteen merchant vessels had been sunk.

Icelanders were warned that it was dangerous to stay out after dark, because of German air raids. When the Icelandic ambassador to the US made a brief visit to Iceland in October, he reported that during his conversations with Roosevelt the president had mentioned these raids and expressed his sorrow over them.

During October 1942, German aircraft made frequent flights over Iceland. In a twenty-day period from October 11, twenty incidents were reported. Raids were often carried out by lone aircraft, and occasionally by small squadrons. They were met with anti-aircraft fire. On October 24, a Condor aircraft was pursued and shot down. The next day, a Junker crashed into the sea near Hvalfjörður, and in the following days, three more German planes were reportedly lost during raids on Iceland, probably also in the sea. Scores of German pilots lost their lives during these surveillance and reconnaissance flights to Iceland.

During autumn 1942, there were complaints in the Reykjavík press about rat infestations in the city. At the same time, in New York, the Daily Record reported a slump in sales of party dresses in the city's department stores. Orders from Iceland kept the US sewing industry afloat.

Convoy SC 107 left New York with 45 merchant ships and 22 escort vessels. Off the coast of Newfoundland, Allied fighter aircraft repelled German U-boats preparing to attack the convoy, sinking two. On November 2, the convoy became separated from its escort and the attacks commenced: nine ships were sunk and three badly damaged. The following day two more ships were sunk, and a further four the day after that. The last ship to come under fire was the Daleby. The captain of an Icelandic vessel, the Brúarfoss, which was next in the convoy, disobeyed the convoy commander's orders, and approached the Daleby. He asked for volunteers, and two crewmen and a passenger made two trips in a lifeboat in heavy seas to the sinking vessel. They rescued 47 men from the ship and the surrounding wreckage. The passenger who had volunteered had twice been in danger of losing his life when he was cast adrift after his ship went down, once on a piece of flotsam and the second time in a lifeboat. A total of 417 men from Convoy SC 107 were rescued and taken to Iceland.

Since the elections in autumn 1942, the Icelandic government had been in crisis, and it seemed unlikely that the parliamentary parties would be able to form a majority government. The previous year, the governor had prepared for the eventuality of an "extra-parliamentary government", and in that situation he felt he had no other choice. A government was formed of civil servants and leading figures in commerce and trade. Their main task, as they saw it, was to halt inflation and implement a price freeze, together with other measures designed to stop the endless price rises. They proposed to increase taxes and improve the supervision of tax collection – both unpopular measures that elected MPs had avoided, or refused to address.

For several years, young Icelandic men had been carrying out acts of vandalism and petty theft. The situation reached a climax when, in early 1943, a gang of youths responsible for a series of break-ins and burglaries was apprehended. In the ringleader's diaries, they discovered that he had planed various crimes from robbing people and killing them, to blackmail and death threats. He and his gang members underwent psychiatric assessments.

Every New year's Eve there was mayhem at the Reykjavík police station, and the fire services spent all night putting out fires. On New Year's night 1942, the police used high-pressure water guns to disperse crowds in the city centre. This was the first time such devices had been used in Iceland.

A quarrel was brewing between Icelandic trawler owners and the British government, who were demanding that fish be delivered not only to cities on the west coast of Great Britain but also to the east coast. This would add several days to the journey and would require more ice to keep the fish fresh, and therefore would lead to a smaller catch and reduced profits. Also, sailing east was considered risky. Fishermen wanted trawlers to be armed for their own safety, and equipped to demagnetise mines in the shipping lanes. By then, the British government was demanding a shipwarrant for small and large vessels. The previous year, Icelandic ships carrying cargoes of iced fish had made over 300 separate journeys to the British Isles. Well into 1943, the Icelandic government negotiated escorts of two or more vessels for these ships, and decreed that transportations should be organised by the association of fishing vessel owners.

In early February 1943, a slow convoy of over 60 vessels and nine escort ships was en route to Liverpool via Iceland, where some of the vessels were bound. On February 5, four more escort ships

US Army encampment on Eyjafjallajökull January 10. The barracks were a long way from the towns, so equipment and provisions had to be transported on horseback. In 1944, the camp was buried under snow and never found again.

Reconnaissance photograph of moorings in Hvalfjörður taken from a German aircraft February 4.

from Hvalfjörður joined the convoy. That same day, the first ship was sunk. The crew of 77 escaped into lifeboats, but were lost at sea. The following day a Polish ship was sunk, and all 36 men on board died. After that a Greek vessel went down. A German U-boat picked up two of its crew, but there is no record of how many perished. In the early hours of February 7, five more vessels were sunk. Soon after, the supply ship, USS Henry R. Mallory, carrying 494 crew and passengers was torpedoed. The ship, which took 30 minutes to sink, was carrying ten lifeboats. One hundred and seventy-five people managed to escape in three of the lifeboats. A nearby vessel was prohibited from going to the scene, and four hours later it was reported that the ship had sunk. Two hundred and thirty-five people were rescued and 272 lost their lives. Twenty U-boats took part in the attack, which resulted in the sinking of 11 vessels. Upwards of 600 merchant sailors lost their lives. A month later, Convoy SC 121 was attacked in the same area with a loss of 14 vessels and 466 merchant sailors.

Nurses having a snowball fight. The photograph was distributed to US newspapers for propaganda purposes.

Numerous survivors were taken to Iceland, both to Reykjavík and Hvalfjörður.

Images from the rescue of the crew of the USS Henry R. Mallory.

During the period of the occupation, the majority of hospital beds were army hospital beds: when the British first arrived, they commandeered schools and halls of residence, and small infirmaries were set up in various locations. A hospital ship was anchored in Akureyri harbour. The Norwegians set up a hospital in Reykjavík, but the Americans went one further. In Helgafell, near Reykjavík, they had 1,000 hospital beds, and it is estimated that at the beginning of 1943, US hospital beds numbered around 2,600. At that time there 1,200 British troops and 37,000 US troops were stationed in Iceland.

An incident occurred just after New Year 1943, of which little was said, although it is recorded in army logbooks. Late one night, on January 27, a homemade bomb was discovered in front of Hótel Borg in Reykjavík. The fuse had burned out before it could detonate the explosive. This was the most serious case of sabotage against the occupying forces. Military intelligence investigated the incident.

A few days later, in the early evening, an explosion occurred in one of the main shopping streets of the capital. A merchant sailor was injured in the blast and died the next day. Shrapnel from the bomb was collected, and it was found to be a signal flare, probably taken from a trawler.

A US Sergeant was found dead in his bed, the murder-weapon a .30 calibre rifle. A forensic firearms examiner was brought over to Iceland to investigate the incident. There is no record of his findings among army files.

Within the space of a month, two aircraft were lost during ferry flights. One crashed after overshooting a runway, and the other while executing an emergency landing, after losing its bearings and running out of fuel. The crew jettisoned all loose objects in the aircraft to lighten the load. The same day, two aircraft suffered damaged during landing.

Ferry flights would land both at Reykjavík and at the new airfields on the Reykjanes peninsula. The airfield at Kaldaðarnes was also still in use. During the winter of 1942–1943, heavy snow in southern Iceland closed mountain roads for six weeks. A pattern of changeable weather followed, with alternating rain and freezing conditions. Ölfusá, the river by the Kaldaðarnes airfield, became blocked with ice, and the river started to overflow. On the evening of March 6, it burst its banks and by midnight the entire airfield was flooded. Nissen huts stood in water and the surrounding current was so powerful that the men had to hold hands to assist each other onto dry land. When daylight came, boats arrived to rescue the men and their belongings. Aircraft from Reykjavík tried unsuccessfully to break up the ice to enable the river to flow. A fleet of fifty trucks arrived, and the soldiers were moved out. The journey across the snowed up mountain roads took over six hours. At the end of April, troops were moved back to Kaldaðarnes, but by summer only a few remained, and by the end of 1943 the barracks at Kaldaðarnes were deserted. The British Army troops were posted back to Great Britain, where a terrible fate awaited them after D-Day. Many would be killed.

Soldiers fleeing the barracks at Kaldaðarnes.

The airfield and the barracks at Kaldaðarnes flooded.

Once Kaldaðarnes was no longer functional, the Reykjanes airfields became all-important. Ground was cleared to make way for two 1,600-metre-long runways: Patterson Airport, named after the pilot, John Gordon Patterson, whose plane went down off the coast of Álftanes. The work was carried out in shifts, with huge bulldozers the like of which had never been seen before in Iceland. The airfield was ready for use by September 1942, and consisted in the end of three 1,500-metre-long runways and parking ramps large enough to accommodate 48 fighter planes, six heavy bombers and 14 cargo planes. By then, ferry flights had been using the airport for almost a month.

The next airfield to be constructed was named after a US pilot called George Meeks, who was also killed in Iceland. A shortage of labour required foreign workers to be brought in from abroad. In the winter of 1943, 3,000 men were employed in building the airfield, which boasted four 2,000-metre-long runways. Major-General Bonesteel inaugurated Meeks Airport on March 24 1943. It was estimated that around 250 ferry flights to the British Isles touched down there every 24 hours.

B-17 ready for take off at Meeks Airport on March 23.

The ban on marriages between soldiers and Icelandic women was still in force when news of Heiða Þorkelsdóttir and Chester T. Swalm's wedding was published in the American press. Many marriages had already taken place between Icelandic women and British and Norwegian soldiers, as well as merchant sailors. Later on, both Heiða and her sister Margrét moved to the States.

Relations between soldiers and local Icelandic women were a contentious issue, and it was not uncommon for women to be denounced for fraternising with soldiers. Matters weren't helped by the endless reports in the press about attacks on women and attempted muggings in the hours of darkness. The military police and the Icelandic police worked together to solve such cases.

A young Icelandic woman living in Copenhagen was sentenced for hiding her German-Jewish lover. He had been wandering from country to country since 1937. She sheltered him, and gave birth to his son in late 1940. The Danish authorities arrested him in February 1941 and deported him in March 1943. The following April, he was sent on a death train to Auschwitz.

In 1934, a young German seamstress called Johanne Goldstein went to work in Iceland, where she lived happily. A year later her mother moved there with her grandson. Threatened with deportation, Johanne married an Icelandic socialist in 1938, and in the autumn of that year her brother also fled to Iceland. The following summer his girlfriend arrived. Another brother, Siegbert, remained in Berlin with his wife and child. Johanne and her family did everything they could to bring him over to Iceland, but to no avail. Siegbert and his family were deported to Auschwitz on March 12 1943. His wife and child were killed on arrival in the camp. Siegbert Goldstein lived on there for five months, before being moved to Natzweiler Struthof, where, together with 85 other men and women, he was killed after being subjected to horrific medical experiments.

In 1943, on the Saturday before Easter, a German Junker Ju 88 with a crew of four left Solna airport on a reconnaissance flight to Iceland. The Junker was spotted off the south coast. Despite thick, low clouds over Reykjavík, several Allied fighter planes took off in pursuit of the Junker. As the two planes exchanged fire, the skies cleared, and both the Junker and the fighter planes were clearly visible from land. The fighter planes fired continuously at the Junker for five minutes until their ammunition was spent. The Junker finally crashed onto the lava fields, halfway between Hafnarfjörður and Keflavík. From the land, a man in a parachute was seen to leap from the falling aircraft.

Mynarek's identity papers. He was 22 years old and decorated with the Iron Cross.

Two boys from a nearby farm made their way towards the crash site, and encountered a man in bare feet brandishing a white flag. He gave them chocolate, and then they led him to the road, where they tried to flag down passing vehicles. Finally, an army truck from the cable laying division stopped, and picked up the German pilot. Another local boy had set off towards the wreckage. He met with six soldiers, who were also out searching, and guided them to the site, where they discovered three dead bodies. One man had tried to bail out of the aircraft, but his parachute had jammed. The pilot who survived was called Anton Mynarek, a 22-year old radio operator and air gunner. He was deported to a prison camp in the US, and his capture was used for propaganda purposes.

In the afternoon of May 3, a Liberator B–24 D aircraft was approaching Iceland in bad weather. Visibility was forty feet, and at 15h00 the crew lost all radio contact. There were fifteen men on board, none of whom had ever been to Iceland: amongst them were Lieutenant Maxwell Andrews, who had taken over as commander of US troops in Europe two months earlier, Chief of Staff Charles H. Barth, Chief of Chaplains Office Frank L. Miller, and other army personnel and flight crew. They were going to Iceland as part of an inspection tour, and to meet with commanders of the Allied forces there.

The aircraft made an abortive attempt to land, but had to climb again. It flew out beyond the Reykjanes peninsula then circled back towards the airfield, attempting an approach from the east. At 16h15 it crashed into a mountain ridge north of Grindavík. The plane was ripped apart in the collision and burst into flames, which the rain soon put out. Trapped in the tail wreckage was the only survivor, air gunner George Eisel. Two of the engines were ripped off the wings during the crash. Eisel waited for 26 hours before he was rescued.

When the aircraft didn't appear, a search party was sent out. Two men from a town on the coast saw the crashed plane, and raised the alarm. They guided a group of soldiers towards the site. By then patrol aircraft had spotted the wreckage from the sky. The British

One of the dead pilots in the wreckage, before the bodies were covered up.

search party was ordered to turn back, but their guides continued to the wreckage and found Eisel still alive. The approach was treacherous, and it took the men an hour to free Eisel from the wreckage, after which he was carried the long way down to a waiting ambulance. Eisel had fought in Africa, and had shot down seven enemy aircraft. He had already escaped death on a previous occasion, when he survived a crash in which three of his fellow airmen died. The bodies of the dead were wrapped in parachutes and flown to Reykjavík. The funeral took place a few days later at Reykjavík Cathedral.

The massif to the east of the Reykjanes airfields continued to be a danger to inexperienced pilots. On June 10, an RAF Hudson aircraft crashed close to Grindavík, with the loss of all five crew.

*Military police officers from the occupying forces salute the
coffins of the dead pilots as they are carried out of the church.*

Social problems were a challenge to the Icelandic authorities
during the war years, but misdemeanours among youths were on
the decrease, and a special home was set up to deal with problem
teenagers. Sixty-one families were under the supervision of social
services, and sexually promiscuous underage girls were fostered
at homes located far from the city. Housing and labour shortages
were ongoing problems in Reykjavík.

The Royal Navy organised a rescue division lead by Icelanders.
Their role was to assist vessels with engine trouble, or which had
run aground. One evening, they were called to Reykjavík harbour,
after a huge explosion occurred in a warehouse. Among the debris
were a number of gas canisters. A cigarette ember was thought to
have caused the blast. There were no casualties.

The governor reminded the parties in government that the US and Great Britain were almost certain to request continued facilities in Iceland after the end of the war, and suggested that it was necessary for the political parties to consider the future defence of the nation. In the autumn 1943, a US congressman made a speech emphasising the urgent need for America to maintain military bases in key locations after the war. Iceland was one of them.

US army reinforcements arrived at the airfields on Reykjanes, and were installed there. Troop carriers took a number of soldiers to the States on leave and on new assignments.

Off the north coast of Iceland, a coaster, the Súðin, came under attack by German aircraft. Two members of the crew were killed and seven wounded. A British trawler went to the ship's rescue, and towed back to the harbour.

A German Focke-Wulf was sighted in the same area, and fighter planes from Akureyri pursued and shot down the aircraft, which crashed into the sea. The crew escaped into a dinghy.

Shots fired from fighter planes overhead prevented a fishing boat from Grímsey from going to their assistance. The crew was moved to the States, where their capture was widely publicised.

In the summer of 1943, disagreements arose among the parliamentary parties in Iceland over plans to found a republic, scheduled for the end of the year. Many

Crewmembers from the German plane given a tour by a MP.

members wished to press ahead with Iceland's independence from Denmark and the Danish crown. A group of intellectuals who opposed the move argued that the country should wait until the end of the war, that while Denmark was still in enemy hands, forming a breakaway republic was incongruous. Opinion polls suggested that just under half of Icelanders considered the project should be shelved until the end of the war. Around 45% of the population wanted to separate from the Danes at the earliest opportunity.

During that year, vast amounts of flotsam from damaged or sunk vessels washed up on Iceland's shores. Locals mostly foraged for driftwood, but occasionally foodstuffs and containers of liquid would also wash up. People were tempted to drink anything in barrels. However, some of it was lethal. That summer, during a national festival on the Westmann Islands, salvaged spirits thought to be methanol were passed around. Methanol is extremely toxic, and nine men died from poisoning both during and after the festival.

The medical division of the US Army built a large hospital with 150 beds in Vogar, on Vatnsleysuströnd in the summer of 1943. The hospital was expanded the following year to encompass 32 buildings and 200 employees. Patients with serious diseases were shipped back to the States for treatment. After D-Day they were flown out. The hospital in Vogar continued being operational until the spring of 1946. A fire that started in the kitchens was spread fast by strong winds, and within hours a large section of the hospital had burned to the ground. The losses were estimated at half a million dollars.

GERMAN SPIES

A German landowner and agricultural engineer named Helmut Lotz who had lived in Iceland from 1928-1930 worked as agent for German Naval Intelligence. Alongside Danish agents of the Nazis in Copenhagen, he sought to recruit young Icelandic men, many of whom men lived in straitened circumstances. He would tempt them with generous offers and grand projects, and propose to pay for trips home. He targeted students in Munich and Berlin first, and when that didn't work he went to Copenhagen. The SS secret services had already enlisted a young Icelander there, whom they had sent to Berlin to train as a radio operator. Lotz found a young student of veterinary medicine, and offered to pay his passage to Iceland.

Helmut Lotz.

In the summer of 1943, another Abwehr agent working in Stettin had recruited a young truck driver, a student of photography, who worked as a cameraman. His mission would be to travel to Iceland where he would send weather reports. As on previous occasions, a submarine took him to Iceland. After he was put ashore on the north east coast, he went straight to the nearest town and handed himself in. Two Icelandic lieutenants from the US Army picked him up. He sat for a month in a Reykjavík prison, before being sent to England, where he was interrogated for two months then taken back to Iceland in a corvette. He arrived in Reykjavík in November. The British strategy was to have two double agents working for them in Reykjavík. And so, Ib Riis and the young photographer both sent out daily, synchronised weather reports, each unaware of the other's existence.

Towards the end of April 1944, two young Icelanders in Copenhagen were preparing to travel to Iceland under the auspices of the Abwehr. Both intended to play a double game, and hand themselves over to the authorities as soon as they arrived. They set off in a boat, claiming they would make land on the northern shores of the Westfjords. Instead, they threw their transmitters overboard, and sailed towards the northeast coast. However, as they approached Raufarhöfn their boat became icebound. The coastguards didn't think the vessel looked suspicious, but when some locals sailed out to them, they were unconvinced by their story, and alerted the authorities. The two young men were taken to Great Britain and separated; one was taken to an interrogation centre, the notorious Camp 020, where he was detained until the end of the war, while the other was sent to hospital suffering from a severe case of tuberculosis. From there he was sent to a prison camp on the Isle of Man.

The next men to be recruited as spies by agents of the Abwehr had gone to Germany to work. They were taken to Iceland by submarine, and put ashore in the northeast. They also handed themselves over to the authorities, were taken to the UK and detained at Camp 020 until autumn 1945.

On the same day in April 1944 when the two men who became icebound outside Raufarhöfn were arrested, the last group of spies working for the Germans under Helmut Lotz set off for Iceland. They included two Icelandic sailors, and a German gardener who had lived in Iceland for twelve years, but had moved back to Germany in 1938. The Abwehr had had these men in their sights for almost two years. They were taken to Iceland by submarine, and were supposed to make land in the north-eastern corner of the island. However, the submarine sailed south to avoid a British destroyer, and they were put ashore there. They wandered around in bad weather for six days, until someone spotted them and alerted the authorities. An American army platoon picked them up, and they were sent to Camp 020 in Great Britain. During their interrogation, they declared that their contact was a young veterinary doctor, the very student Lotz had enlisted during Germany's earliest attempts to set up a spy ring. All three men were detained until August 1945.

Accidents in and around the island involving British, Norwegian and American aircraft were numerous. Within a two-month period, four Mitchell II B–25 bombers and a Boeing B-17G were lost with 30 men on board. Two Hudson FK/768s also went down during that time, one crashed into the sea, and the other overshot a runway; in the first crash five men died and in the second all survived.

Firefighters at work on a plane on fire at Patterson Airport.

In November 1943, the hot springs around Reykjavík finally brought central heating to the majority of the city's inhabitants. The project had begun in the summer of 1940. Large areas of Reykjavík remained dug up for weeks and months on end while pipes were being laid, which lead to an increased danger of road accidents. In his memoirs, Churchill claimed the idea was his, but preparations had been going on for years. Finally, just before war broke out, the contract was given to Danish engineers who designed the system, which was financed with loans from a Danish bank. The arrival of central heating changed the appearance of

*An American diner at the Red Cross-facilities in Reykjavík.
The US Red Cross was in charge of running dancehalls and
cinemas for the army, to the dismay of many Icelanders*

Reykjavík; the black coal smoke hovering above the city vanished, and with it the acrid smell.

There was a surplus of food in Iceland, a lot of which was thrown away, including meat and fish, some of it spoiled due to lack of adequate cold storage. There was much discussion the autumn of 1943 about contributing aid to the war torn countries of Europe.

Over the New Year, two Icelandic men found themselves in Sachsenhausen concentration camp. One of them had recently arrived from Berlin, where he was married to a German woman, and had ended up working in the black market. The other, a young retailer, was arrested in Norway as he was preparing to flee to Sweden. The black marketeer died at the beginning of 1944.

After conquering Salerno, the Americans liberated a POW camp in Campio. A young Icelandic woman was released who had been detained there in atrocious conditions for over three years.

In the summer of 1943, a young Icelander was arrested in Norway. In the New Year he was transported to the Natzweiler-Struthof concentration camp in Germany, where he died of hunger the following March.

Other Icelanders found themselves caught up in war zones. Many Icelandic women were living in Germany, and some of them had children. It was common for Icelandic men to seek work in Germany where there was a shortage of manpower in the years before the war. Some joined the SS: one was a guard at Dora-Mittelbau concentration camp, where V2 rockets were manufactured, another worked as an SS combat engineer on the Eastern front, and a third worked in the propaganda department of the SS; he was the Governor of Iceland Sveinn Björnsson's eldest son.

SS El Grillo sinking in Seyðisfjörður.

After the 1943 bombings of the harbour, air defences in Seyðis-fjörður were strengthened. An electronic radar system and larger anti-aircraft guns were installed. During an air drill on January 10, three Focke-Wulf aircraft were detected at 12,000 feet. While soldiers attempted to train the anti-aircraft guns on them, the mechanism jammed. The aircraft dropped five bombs, two of them close to SS El Grillo, a 7,000-ton oil tanker carrying 9,000 tons of fuel oil. The ship started taking in water. The crew was moved to safety, and shortly afterwards, the ship sank. It is believed that the British scuppered her rather than risk another air attack. A few months later, three German aircraft bombed the area. The wreck still lies in 50 metres of water, and has leaked small amounts of fuel, although most of it has been syphoned out of the tanks.

Nissen huts: The severe housing shortage in Reykjavík led to homeless Icelandic families squatting in dilapidated Nissen huts in abandoned barracks. The Reykjavík health authorities urged families to move out of the worst ones, although the alternative accommodation they were offered wasn't much of an improvement. For some of the city's poorest families, the Nissen huts in Reykjavík went on providing a solution to homelessness well into the fifties. Women made pregnant by soldiers who were subsequently posted overseas – the "soldiers' wives" – were among the first to take over the huts.

Mama's Café. A woman showing some US officers Icelandic beer. She is wearing her Sunday best, the traditional Icelandic women's dress, which in fact dates from the 1800's. The woman's name was Guðlaug Björnsdóttir, and she was born in Fljót. She moved to Reykjavík, where, after losing her husband in a traffic accident in 1939, she was left to bring up two young children on her own. When the occupation began, she opened a restaurant in a shack on Suðurlandsbraut in Reykjavík – Mama's Café – which quickly became a favourite haunt of soldiers from the nearby barracks in Laugardalur: she served mostly eggs, and chips, but her friendliness was what made the place popular. Her son decided to join the US Army, and moved to the States, and when Guðlaug lost her only daughter, he became mother to her daughter's five children.

Early in 1944, the US Army changed the rules outlawing marriage between soldiers and Icelandic women, and the first weddings were held in March of that year.

At the end of March, the head of the US military police held a press meeting in an attempt to clarify the army's position. He considered relations between the army and the civilian population harmonious. In his view, a small group of Icelanders were the troublemakers, and the military police constantly came up against the same individuals.

*The US Red Cross organised a "March collection
fund", and also ran a social club for soldiers.*

Around that time, the US forces set up their own radio station, initially with equipment gathered from various sources – the
transmitter was retrieved from the wreckage of a German aircraft
that had been shot down. The station could be picked up at the
US army bases, and played mostly music. The British Army had
been given access to state radio transmissions from the very beginning of the occupation, but the American radio station would
continue broadcasting right up until the start of the 21st century.

The economy was undergoing momentous changes, best
exemplified by the amount of money in circulation: at the end
of 1939 this stood at around 13.5 million Icelandic krona. By the
beginning of 1944, it had increased tenfold. Some months before
the founding of the Icelandic republic, articles appeared in the
British press criticising the prosperity in this affluent country of

In the years leading up to D-Day, leisure activities of the occupying forces were diverse, and would have a long-lasting effect on the nation's way of life. The arrival of magazines from the US containing stories of Hollywood and its stars was eagerly awaited. Comics became the daily fodder of children and teenagers. Swing music and the jitterbug swept the dance floors. New sports such as basketball, bowling and boxing caught on.

"callous, greedy people". They expressed shock at the exorbitant cost of goods, and claimed that only food could be purchased at reasonable prices.

Financiers were alarmed at the level of personal savings, which by the New Year 1944 had soared to 452 million krona, while the amount of money Icelandic banks had invested abroad stood at 447 million krona. It was estimated that by the end of the year Icelandic funds in British and American banks would be equvalent to 600 million kronas. In 1939 individual savings in Iceland had amounted to 89 million krona.

As the year 1944 went on, fierce disputes erupted over the question of Icelandic independence, and those who advocated postponing the foundation of the republic were defeated. Their cause wasn't helped by the message King Christian X sent to the Icelandic government, against the recommendation of his advisors, which arrived on May 4. In it the Danish king made clear his opposition to Iceland founding a republic, and declared that he would refuse to recognise it. The response of the government and of Iceland's political parties was dispatched the following day. A republic would be founded, and a modified constitution drawn up, subject to the will of the people to be determined in a general election. This took place on May 20, with an unparalleled turnout of 98.61%, which in some places rose to 100%. Ninety-seven percent of the population agreed to the dissolution of the Act of Union, and 95% with the founding of a republic. Preparations for Iceland's birth as an independent republic on June 17 were gathering momentum.

The Danish king was informed of the results of the election at the beginning of June, and this time the last King of Iceland yielded to the entreaties of his advisors – amongst them Danish politicians, Queen Alexandra, and King Gus-

The emblem of the independence festivities.

taf of Sweden: by June 16, his farewell speech and welcoming address to the new republic had been composed.

Readings of Icelandic weather reports caused Eisenhower to delay by 24 hours the Normandy landings, which finally commenced at midnight on June 6 1944 with an airborne contingent and approximately 5,000 amphibious vessels. Few people were aware that many Icelanders from Canada and the United States took part in the landings, both in the marines and the engineer corps that came behind. Two lost their lives on the first day, and a third the day after. During the week that followed, they would fall one by one alongside their fellow soldiers: two in Caen, and others in unknown locations in France, Belgium and Holland. There were a similar number of fatalities in Iceland: from the end of April to the end of June 1944 upwards of thirty men died in air crashes.

Þingvellir June 17 1944. Parliament in session as independence is declared in rainy weather. Foreign visitors came from the United Kingdom, the United States of America, the Soviet Union, Free France and the Nordic countries.

The festivities were continued in Reykjavík on June 18 in much better weather. In the evening there was a banquet at Hótel Borg with dignitaries.

On June 17 1944, Iceland declared its independence on a rainy day in Þingvellir before a crowd of thousands. Parliament elected the first president of the republic by a sweeping majority. Later that day, a message of goodwill from the Danish king was read out to the crowd, who received it with cries of jubilation.

Foreign diplomats attended the celebrations, which continued in Reykjavík and throughout the country for several days. The newly appointed US ambassador delivered a formal invitation from Roosevelt to the new Icelandic president. The strength of the Red Army was a source of great concern to the Americans, and the US ambassador conveyed these fears during a meeting with the Icelandic Foreign Secretary, Vilhjálmur Þór, former consul in New York, who had been lobbying for US military protection for his country in 1939. The newly elected president now prepared for his first official visit to Washington.

On the eve of his departure, a stir was caused by reports of a statement by the chairman of the US Senate Foreign Relations Committee regarding the urgent need for America to retain a military base on Icelandic soil. Most newspapers stated that the emphatic will of the people was to begin the history of their young republic without the presence of foreign military bases.

The president of Iceland spent his first night at the White House, and then moved to the President's Guest House, known as Blair House. He was given a respectful welcome. After laying a wreath on the Tomb of the Unknown Soldier in Arlington Cemetery, he visited the US Congress and made a trip to Mount Vernon. He and his entourage then went on to New York, where he was met by Mayor La Guardia. During his visit to the States, members of the Icelandic parliament rejected the idea of the US Army remaining in Iceland.

Roosevelt and Sveinn Björnsson in the Oval Office. After a three day stay in Washington the president travelled to New York for a two day visit.

An installation for a photo shoot for personal greetings cards for Christmas 1944. The pair in the front seats is unknown, but in the back seats are Chester Penko and his fiancée, Olga Dagmar Nielsen, one of three sisters who all married US servicemen and moved to the States after the war.

There was great unrest that autumn in Denmark, and many demonstrations. An armed insurrection broke out in and around the Royal Palace during which several German soldiers were killed. The Danish police force was dissolved, and those who didn't go into hiding were rounded up and sent to Neuengamme concentration camp. At that time, SS member Björn Sv. Björnsson was working in the propaganda department of the German occupying forces. He was ordered to take over the state radio, which he did for 10 days. Björn Sv. Björnsson became the focus of broadcasts on the radio station run by the Free Danes in London, amongst whom was the son of a close colleague of President Sveinn Björnsson from his years as ambassador to Denmark and advisor to the Danish king: President Sveinn Björnsson was Björn Sv. Björnsson's father. This situation became something of a headache for the Icelandic authorities. At the same time, the Icelandic prime minister's nephew was being detained by the British on charges of espionage in Iceland; he had been among those the Abwehr sent there the previous year.

A veterinarian returned from Sweden to Iceland via Prestwick in Scotland, where he was arrested, taken to London and held in custody. On the third day, he was interrogated, and accused of heading a German espionage network in Iceland. Finally, Helmut Lotz's interest in the young student of veterinary medicine a few years earlier had been uncovered. The veterinarian was detained in Camp 020 until August 1945. During his captivity, he shared a dormitory with high-ranking German officials such as SS second-in-command Kaltenbrunner, who tried to engage him in conversation. However, it seemed the young vet had no interest in making their acquaintance.

Björn Sv. Björnsson was the oldest son of Sveinn Björnsson, born in 1909. As a young man he was a gifted musician, but got 15 year-old girl pregnant at the age of 19 and his parents decided it was best for the young couple to stay abroad. Björn was employed by the Icelandic Steamship Company in Hamburg that his father had founded years earlier. Björn was very early taken by the politics of the National Socialists in Germany. He started his own company in imports-exports but went bankrupt after three years in 1938. His marriage dissolved and he returned to Denmark. In August 1941 he enrolled in Waffen SS. He was trained in Breslau, but after that got a special training as reporter, after which he was sent to the Eastern front following Divison Wiking, the nordic part of the SS. In November 1943 he was transferred to a SS Standarte propaganda unit in Copenhagen.

Skeena stranded at Viðey. The oil spill is clear on the picture.

On October 23 1944, the Canadian destroyer HMCS Skeena was caught in a fierce storm while moored off Reykjavík, and ran aground close to the island of Viðey with 213 men on board. The ship's fuel tanks were ripped open on the rocks, and leaking fuel formed into oil slicks, which were tossed about by the waves, covering both the ship and the crew. Two life rafts carrying 21 men cast off and disappeared into the darkness. A rescue boat attempted an approach, but was forced to turn back. The head lifeguard ordered a landing boat to be brought, and he and his team sailed round to the northern side of island. They put ashore, and walked to where the Skeena had run aground. A rope was cast out to the ship, and for two hours or more, the head lifeguard stood in the surf up to his waist, receiving the men from the stranded vessel one by one. Further north, the two life rafts had reached the shore, where the men lay in blackened heaps on the shore. One of them managed to get to the nearest farm, and the other survivors were picked up. The following day, it was discovered that 15 men had lost their lives. Allegedly there was a danger of possible multiple explosions on the stranded Skeena. The army ordered a news blackout over the incident, which was kept under wraps for almost a quarter of a century.

In November 1944, U-boats torpedoed an American oil tanker off the coast of Reykjavík. Sailing in the same convoy was a passenger ship, the Goðafoss, also on its way from the States. Flouting orders, the captain of the passenger ship went to the aid of the oil tanker. Many of the tanker's crew were rescued, but three hours later the Goðafoss was hit by a torpedo and sank within minutes. Twenty-five people lost their lives and 19 survived. Later that day, a tugboat was sent out on a search mission, but vanished with everyone on board. Seventy-two people lost their lives that day close to Reykjavík, among them several women, one of whom was pregnant, as well as four young children who were on their way home.

Christmas in a hospital in Iceland. The photo was published around Christmas 1941 and distributed prior to the festivities a year later.

At the beginning of the year 1945, British and American diplomats held secret talks with the Icelandic ambassadors to London and Washington about the possibility of basing the United Nations headquarters in Reykjavík.

There was little news from Norway, which was still under the German yoke. In collaboration with the Norwegian Red Cross, a collection for the people of Norway began in Iceland in November. Money was raised to pay for a hundred tons of cod liver oil capsules, which were sent to Norway via the Red Cross. Large amounts of clothing were also collected, as well as 10,000 pounds sterling for the purchase of drugs and medical equipment.

During discussions between the Icelandic and British authorities, it was revealed that 75% of all fish imports to Great Britain during the war had come from Iceland.

Icelandic imports of American goods came under investigation, and it emerged that twelve wholesale firms had set up branches in the US, where they raised the price of goods before shipping them to Iceland, enabling them to accumulate money in US banks. Those involved were prosecuted.

With the offensive on mainland Europe the activities of the US Army in Iceland slowed down, and the Icelandic authorities began discussions with the military over the purchase of machinery, equipment and installations belonging to or constructed by the occupying forces. These negotiations would take almost five years.

Local authorities decided to include in their budgets alimony payments for women with children fathered by soldiers who had subsequently left the country. A demand was made to the state for these payments to be reimbursed. Many years after the war ended, the question of paternity remained an issue for many people. The Red Cross acted as a mediator to resolve these cases wherever they could, but there are still some Icelanders alive today who have never found their fathers.

On January 24 1945, a U-boat attacked an Icelandic merchant vessel off the coast of Belfast. The ship went down in seven minutes, taking 15 men with it. Twenty-eight men survived. A month later, a British patrol vessel was sunk in Faxaflói, and of the 26 crewmembers only one escaped with his life. A third ship was sunk in the same area on March 28, a cargo vessel with a crew of 38. Three were killed in the attack, and eight others were wounded but survived.

At a meeting in Crimea of the great powers, eight members of the Associated Nations were invited to become founding members

A group of women saying goodbye to soldiers leaving for the States. Many of the soldiers would go to the Pacific to fight.

of the United Nations, providing they agreed to declare war on Germany and Japan. A majority in the Icelandic parliament voted against the motion, and requested to be granted a special status. The United States, Great Britain and the Soviet Union refused, and so the Icelandic republic was not a founding member of the UN in San Francisco.

Folke Bernadotte and Heinrich Himmler arranged for prisoners in German prison camps from the Nordic countries to

Leifur Müller. His index card from Sachsenhausen.

A German JU-88 A-6/U from Bardufoss in Norway with a experienced crew of four crashed in the northeast of Iceland on May 2. One wing was torn from the plane in the landing.

be transported in 178 white coaches to Neuengamme concentration camp outside Hamburg. The Danish Red Cross supplied 123 extra vehicles. One man who survived this journey was a young Icelandic retailer who had been imprisoned in Sachsenhausen. Concealed beneath his clothing were several pages of photographs, the only ones that survived of prisoners in Sachsenhausen.

In April, sand bag shelters erected by the British in May 1940 both in Reykjavík and other towns started being dismantled.

The trade office, set up when the US Army took over the defence of the country in July 1941, was shut down. The office had been responsible for locating supplies in America, and also dealt with the British over payments for fish exports to Great Britain. Up until the end of 1943, Iceland had made purchases worth 65 million dollars or 420 million krona. In April of that year, Icelanders had 37 million dollars deposited in US banks.

On May 2 1945, a German aircraft made an emergency landing in northeast Iceland. Four members of the crew survived the crash and surrendered. On the same day, a U-boat sank a British armed trawler off the north coast, from which 23 men died and one survived.

On May 5, a U-boat attacked the Empire Unity. Originally a German vessel, she had been placed under a travel ban in 1939, but managed to flee to the Denmark Strait, where the British captured her and renamed her the Empire Unity. The ship remained afloat and was towed to Hvalfjörður.

That same day, Field Marshal Montgomery's 21st Army Group reached the borders of Germany and Denmark, where Admiral von Friedenburg, who had arrived with the first U-boats to Iceland in the summer of 1939, signed Germany's first surrender of occupied territory.

Denmark was now liberated from German occupation, but the country was still over-run with German soldiers, who now surrendered their weapons and made their way home on foot. A state of lawlessness and unrest continued to reign in Danish towns and cities. During that period, two Icelanders were murdered in Copenhagen. In the weeks that followed, anyone who had collaborated with the German occupying forces was arrested, dragged before the courts and sentenced. Among them were several Icelandic men. One was deported to Norway, where he was sen-

Ólafur Pétursson in a parade with his comrades in the Icelandic Nazy Party.

tenced for betraying members of the Norwegian resistance to the SS. He had informed on the young retailer who spent the war in Sachsenhausen.

THE ACCOUNTANT'S STORY

In 1938, a young Icelander went to Norway to study accountancy. He came from a middle class family in Reykjavík, and had openly declared his support for the Nazi party. In August 1940, a handful of Icelanders stranded in Norway managed to find a small vessel, and, after obtaining a travel permit from the German authorities in Bergen, they sailed home to Iceland. The evening of their departure from the harbour, a group of German intelligence agents arrived uninvited. The young student of accountancy was amongst the Icelanders, and he went ashore with the Germans. They liked the look of this fellow who shared their views, and ended up recruiting him, but he refused to carry out espionage for them in Iceland. His first mission was to smuggle a German spy into Britain disguised as a refugee via Iceland. The man was captured on arrival in Britain, and confessed to what he was doing there and who had helped him get there. The young accountant became a person of interest to British intelligence. In the summer of 1941, he refused a second time to go to Iceland when another ship containing Icelandic refugees left Norway. The German undercover agent who arrived in Britain disguised as a refugee lost his nerve and hanged himself.

The accountant visited coffee shops and restaurants, where he would engage fellow customers in conversation. From mid-1941 until the end of summer 1942, he managed to gain the confidence of men with connections to the Norwegian resistance movement, and he supplied regular information he deemed significant to the German secret services. It is estimated that he was partly responsible for the arrest of up to fifty men. One of those men was executed, 9 died in custody, and 18 remained in prison until the end of the war. The accountant reportedly informed the Germans that a compatriot of his, a young retailer, was planning to flee to Sweden. The young man was arrested and imprisoned in Neuengamme concentration camp and then moved to Sachsenhausen until the end of the war.

By autumn 1942, the accountant's situation was becoming precarious, and he fled to Copenhagen, where he joined the criminal investigation branch of the Danish police. He allegedly continued to collaborate with the Germans. When the Icelandic passenger ship, Esja, arrived in Copenhagen after the German surrender to pick up Icelanders who had spent the war years in Denmark, the accountant's name was on the passenger list. The ship was leaving the harbour, when it was detained. A group of British soldiers went on board and arrested five men. Among them was the young accountant. On September 1 1945, he was deported to Norway as a prisoner, and interrogated by the Norwegian authorities. When the Icelandic authorities began enquiring about his case they received a clear answer: the man had broken several laws, and had possibly committed treason. The court handed down a twenty-year sentence.

Despite his obvious guilt, the Icelandic authorities refused to give up, and made every effort to secure his release from the Norwegian prison. Over the next few years, the diplomatic services persistently demanded the release of this criminal, and finally managed to secure his deportation, although not his acquittal. He arrived home exactly ten years after he had Iceland left to study abroad, dishonoured and despised.

On May 7 1945, the Icelandic president's eldest son, SS member Björn Sv. Björnsson, surrendered to the Danish authorities. Iceland's acting ambassador to Denmark wrote a letter to the authorities pointing out that Björn Sv. Björnsson was an Icelandic national. His mother flew to Stockholm, arriving by train to Copenhagen on May 11. Two days earlier, Björn's lawyer had requested his release, ordering Foreign Minister John Christmas Møller, one of Denmark's foremost leaders during the occupation, to free Björn from prison. However, the British intervened, and took him into custody. On the evening of June 11, Björn's mother met with Møller and his wife over dinner at the Hotel Angleterre. A few weeks earlier, the couple's only son had been killed by a sniper's bullet.

Björn was released from custody on May 18 1946, and that same evening he travelled to Sweden. From there he returned to Iceland. His release had by then made the headlines in Denmark, and he was under investigation by two different departments of Danish government. Björn made a solemn promise to his father not to discuss his career in the SS. He kept that promise until 1989, when he published his memoirs. The book reportedly contains several inaccuracies, and many ambiguities remain about the period he spent serving in the SS on the eastern front.

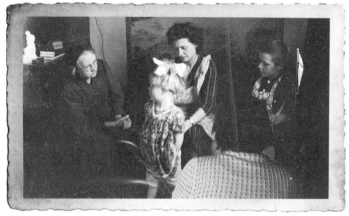

Three generations listen to Churchill declaring Allied victory in Europe on May 8.

VE Day on May 8 1945 was a day of relief and unrest in western countries. In Reykjavík, a procession made its way to the Norwegian and Danish embassies to celebrate the freedom of the two nations from German oppression. British soldiers were celebrating, and crowds of people in their Sunday best filled the city centre. As the evening drew on, there was much drunken revelry, and the police used tear gas on groups of both British and Icelandic men caught committing acts of vandalism. Shots were fired, and it was a miracle no one was hurt. The American soldiers remained confined to their barracks.

Acting on behalf of the authorities, the Red Cross compiled

British soldiers celebrating the victory in Reykjavík.
US soldiers were confined to their barracks.

a register of Icelanders living in Germany and Central Europe. Envoys were then sent to the mainland to bring them home. Among them were students, men, women and children. Many had suffered hardships during the war years; they had been bombed, witnessed fatalities in their hometowns, and been forced to undertake hazardous journeys to flee from war zones. Icelandic fishing vessels started taking fish to Germany again. Sailors were shocked at the devastation wrought upon cities, and their inhabitants. The first to arrive established the custom of donating part of their catch to people begging for food at the harbour.

On July 7 1945, the young retailer who had spent the last years of the war in Sachsenhausen was flown home to Iceland in a military aircraft. He had been under observation by Swedish and Norwegian doctors, and felt unable to share his experiences. With the help of a journalist, he wrote a brief account of his detention there; it was among the first descriptions of life in a Nazi prison camp ever published. Many years later, he rewrote a more exhaustive account, comtaining detailed descriptions.

Ib Riis had led a lonely life in Reykjavík working as a double agent for the British secret services, but in 1942 he met a girl and married her. After the war, they moved to Copenhagen, and ended up settling in the States. He published his memoirs in 1990. A controversy over the disappearance of Convoy PQ 17 escort caused much interest in Great Britain, and the secret services impounded a book that came out in 1969 about the fate of the convoy. In an article published in the *Sunday Times* in 2003, Riis was accused of having played a role in the destruction of Convoy PQ 17. As a result, official files were made public, and Riis received a letter from Her Majesty's Secret Service, acknowledging his contribution, and absolving him of any responsibility for the convoy's fate.

The Royal Navy left Iceland on July 31 1945.

A month later, 31 Icelandic women together with 22 children fathered by American soldiers left for the States. Some of the Jewish refugees who had been given temporary leave to remain in Iceland also left that summer for the States. A few chose to stay, and of those who left, some made a request for their ashes to be returned to Iceland and buried in Icelandic soil. A few Germans who had been deported from Iceland in the spring of 1940 were given leave to return, after a long battle with the Icelandic authorities and the Allied ban on movements in and out of Germany's occupied zones.

Ten men returned to Iceland, after being detained for various lengths of time in British prison camps. They had all been accused of spying for the Germans in Iceland, but some were innocent, and others had been coerced into what were considered to be acts of espionage.

In the summer of 1945, Icelanders donated clothes, many of them children's clothes, to Danes in need. For a long time, Danes resented the way in which Icelanders had dissolved the Act of Union between their two countries, and for the first few years after the war, Icelanders in Denmark were met with animosity.

The war was still going on in the Pacific, but the dropping of atom bombs on Hiroshima and Nagasaki led to the surrender of the Japanese emperor. Soon after the end of the war was announced, ships in Faxaflói close to Reykjavík sounded their horns and people let off fireworks. Crowds took to the streets, which resounded with

US soldiers in front of a crowd of Icelanders a few moments after the victory was announced in the Pacific theatre of war.

the ceaseless peal of church bells. There was great rejoicing among the soldiers and the merchant sailors from all different countries, and they danced together. The following day, flags flew all over the country, and many workplaces granted their employees a holiday.

The state sell-off of vehicles belonging to the occupying forces came under fire; it was rumoured that wealthy individuals acquired large numbers of vehicles on the cheap and sold them on for a profit. The state purchased close to 10,000 Nissen huts and other buildings to the tune of 850,000 krona. Eventually, the Icelandic authorities negotiated with the commanders of the occupying forces to pay 850,000 dollars for army equipment, spare parts and road construction machinery valued at five million US dollars. This did not include a large number of civil works, harbours, roads and airfields worth several millions of dollars, which, according to prior agreements, would revert to the state after the army's departure.

The Icelanders were rich: they had accumulated 563 million krona in savings banks, 428 million of which came from fees paid by the occupying forces for services rendered. No sooner did steel and concrete become readily available than a construction boom commenced in Iceland. Thirty trawlers were commissioned from British shipyards. Icelanders returning from war-torn Europe had difficulty recognising the country they had left six years earlier. Everything had changed.

A peaceful street in Reykjavík, but Icelandic society had undergone drastic changes during the years of occupation.

It is commonly asked how many Icelanders died as a result of "military causes". Of the 2,000 Icelanders resident in North America who served in the British, Canadian or US forces, approximately 110 were killed in mainland Europe, on the Italian Peninsula, and in Africa. Others fell in Burma, Hong Kong and the Pacific.

Official estimates of how many people died in Iceland as a result of "military causes" put the figure at 175. That number doesn't take into account accidents at sea due to unknown causes, or road accidents resulting from radical changes to the traffic system, or the many deaths brought about due to the vast numbers of army vehicles in circulation. Nor does it include the many accidents that took place on the coast, which can be directly attributed to changes wrought by the occupation: lighthouse blackouts, restrictions on weather news' broadcasts, and blacked out vessels navigating the shipping lanes. Whatever the numbers of Icelandic casualties, lots more lives were lost in the seas and skies around and above Iceland. Many soldiers also died in Iceland because of traffic accidents, others died of exposure or because of the harsh terrain, or were drowned in lakes, rivers and coastal regions.

The US authorities had been pleading their case for a long-term military base in Iceland from the moment the president of Iceland first visited Washington in the summer of 1944. But their appeals were largely ignored. On October 1 1945, they ran out of patience: a written message was delivered, outlining the superpower's frontiers, and revealing that Iceland was to be the leading bastion of these frontiers. The US request was disastrous for the Iceland government of the time. The Icelandic authorities clashed with US officials, and the US ambassador to Iceland concealed the situation from his own government. The Icelandic prime minister dared not put the US request to the people of Iceland, and yet he was convinced that the superpower would refuse to take no for an answer. A year later, the American government sent another detailed request, which again was met with a refusal. And yet, within five years, in 1951, the US Army arrived once more on Iceland's shores. They kept a military base there until 2006, when, almost overnight, they disappeared.

PICTURE CREDITS

6. Eðvarð Sigurgeirsson. Akureyri Museum.
7. Ólafur Magnússon. Reykjavík City Museum.
8. Unknown. Getty/Nordic Photos.
9. Unknown. NARA.
10. Unknown. Private Collection.
11. Sigurður Guðmundsson. National Museum of Iceland.
13. Above: National Museum of Iceland. Below: Vigfús Sigurgeirsson.
14. www.uboat.net. Collection of Bill Murray.
15. Vigfús Sigurgeirsson.
19. Unknown. www.freespace.virgin.net.
20. Ívar Guðmundsson.
21. Einar Jónsson.
23. Unknown. Private Collection.
24. August Darvill.
25.–26. Svavar Hjaltested.
28. Above: Sigurhans Vignir. Below: Svavar Hjaltested.
29. Svavar Hjaltested.
30. Svavar Hjaltested.
31. Sigurhans Vignir.
32. Svavar Hjaltested.
33. Unknown. Private Collection.
34. Arnbergur Stefánsson. Borgarnes Museum.
35. Unknown. National Museum of Iceland.
36. August Darvill.
40. Þorsteinn Jósefsson. National Museum of Iceland.
41. Unknown. Private Collection.
45. Unknown. NARA.
46. Unknown. NARA.
48. Unknown. Signal Corps.
49. Unknown. NARA.
50. Above: Unknown. NARA. Below: Þorsteinn Jósefsson. National Museum of Iceland.
51. Unknown. NARA.
52. Unknown. www.uboatarchive.net.
53. Unknown. NARA.
54. Unknown.www.navysource.org.
57. Unknown. www.sheffield-history.co.uk.
59. Above: Unknown. Private Collection. Below: www.biblio.org/hyperwar/ USCG/VIII
60. Unknown. NARA.
61. Unknown. Private Collection.
62. Skafti Guðjónsson. Reykjavík City Museum.
65. Svavar Hjaltested.
66. Unknown. Private Collection.
67. Unknown. Private Collection.
68. Unknown. Fold3.
70. Unknown. Fold3.
74. Above: Unknown. NARA. Below: Unknown. NARA.
76. Hugo Löhr. Private Collection.
77. Unknown. NARA.
79. Unknown. Private Collection.
82. Above: Unknown. Private Collection. Below: Hugo Löhr. Private Collection.
83. Unknown. Signal Corps.
84. Above: Unknown. www.USCGmil. history.com. Below: Unknown. www. USCGmil.history.com.
86. Unknown. Private Collection.
87. Unknown. Private Collection.
88. Unknown. NARA.
89. Private Collection.
91. Unknown. Fold3.
92. Unknown. Private Collection.
93. Unknown. Signal Corps.
94. Unknown. Private Collection.
97. Unknown. Fold3.
98. Unknown. Signal Corps.
99. Ástvaldur Andrésson. Private Collection.
100. Skafti Guðjónsson. Reykjavík City Museum.
101. Unknown. Signal Corps.
102. Unknown. Signal Corps.
103. Above: Unknown. Signal Corps. Below: www.magazinesfamousfix. com.
104. Stefán Jónsson.
105. Sigurður Tómasson. National Museum of Iceland.
106. Kadorian. Signal Corps.
107. Unknown. Private Collection.
108. Unknown. Reykjavík City Museum.
109. Unknown. National Museum of Iceland.
110. Unknown. Private Collection.
111. Unknown. Signal Corps.
113. Above: Unknown. Signal Corps. Below: Registrar: Sachsenhausen. Private Collection
114. Jón Magnússon. Reykjavík City Museum.
115. Unknown. Private Collection.
118. Þór Sandholt. National Museum of Iceland.
119. Svavar Hjaltested.
121. Unknown. Private Collection.
122. Unknown. Signal Corps.
123. Unknown. Signal Corps.

SELECTED BIBLIOGRAPHY

Ásgeir Guðmundson, 1991: *Gagnnjósnari Breta á Íslandi*. Reykjavík. Skjaldborg.

Ásgeir Guðmundsson, 1992: *Eyrnatog og steinbítstak*. Reykjavík. Skjaldborg.

Ásgeir Guðmundsson, 2009: *Berlínarblús*. Reykjavík. Skrudda.

Ásgeir Guðmundsson, Ögmundur Björnsson, 1990: *Með kveðju frá St. Bernharðshundinum*. Reykjavík. Skjaldborg.

Bittner, D. F., 1983: The Lion and the White Falcon. *Britain and Iceland in the World War II era*. BNA. Arcon Books.

Conn, Stetson, Engelman, R. C., Fairchild, Byron, 2000 (1964): *Guarding the United States and its outposts*. United States Army in World War 2. Washington. D.C. Center of Military History, United States Army.

Corgan, Michael Thomas, 1992: "Aðdragandinn vestanhafs að hervernd Bandaríkjamanna á Íslandi 1941." *Saga* 30 (2). Reykjavík. Sögufélagið

Friðþór Eydal, 1999: *Fremsta víglína*. Reykjavík. Bláskeggur.

Friðþór Eydal, 1998: *Vígdrekar og vopnagnýr*. Reykjavík. Bláskeggur.

Friðþór Eydal, 2007: *Frá heimstyrjöld til herverndar*. Keflavíkurstöðin. Reykjavík. Bláskeggur.

Guðmundur Kristinsson, 2002: *Styrjaldarárin á Suðurlandi*. Selfoss. Árnesútgáfan.

Sigurdsson, Jon, 1990: *Veterans of Icelandic Descent*. World War II 1939–1945. Winnipeg, Manitoba. Jon Sigurdsson Chapter IODE.

Magnús Þór Hafsteinsson, 2011: *Dauðinn í Dumbshafi*. Reykjavík. Hólar.

Páll Baldvin Baldvinsson, 2015: *Stríðsárin*. Reykjavík. JPV.

Þór Whitehead, 1980: *Ófriður í aðsigi*. Reykjavík. Vaka-Helgafell.

Þór Whitehead, 1985: *Stríð fyrir ströndum*. Reykjavík. Vaka-Helgafell.

Þór Whitehead, 1999: *Bretarnir koma*. Reykjavík. Vaka-Helgafell.

Þór Whitehead, 1998: *Milli vonar og ótta*. Reykjavík. Vaka-Helgafell.

Þór Whitehead, 2002: *Ísland í hers höndum*. Reykjavík. Vaka-Helgafell.

Þór Whitehead, 2013: "Ástandið og yfirvöldin. Stríðið um konurnar." *Saga* 51 (2). Reykjavík. Sögufélagið.

INDEX